LIFE

THE ROAD TO VJ DAY

ITALIAN AMERICANS WAVED flags and tossed papers from windows in New York City streets to celebrate Japan's unconditional surrender to the Allies—and the end of World War II—on August 14, 1945.

LIFE

The Road to VJ Day

MARINES RACED FOR COVER IN November 1943 while assaulting Betio, a part of the Tarawa Atoll in the Gilbert Islands. One Marine bringing in men aboard a Higgins landing craft commented, "It's hell in there."

CONTENTS

INTRODUCTION

VJ DAY: RELIEF, REJOICING, AND A RECKONING

World War II came to an end 75 years ago, yet the outcome, and the crucial battles waged on the islands of the Pacific, still resonate

BY DANIEL S. LEVY

AS SERVICEMEN AND CIVILIANS awaited President Harry Truman's official announcement of the defeat of the Japanese, they joyfully danced the conga opposite the White House.

ON THE EVENING OF AUGUST 14, 1945, THE words "Official—Truman announces Japanese surrender" streamed around the New York Times Tower's news zipper. President Harry S. Truman's proclamation marking the end of World War II unleashed a wave of communal ecstasy. Before long, some 2 million people packed into Times Square. They tossed hats into the air, cheered, embraced, and cried. From high up in office buildings and hotels, others threw down confetti and streamers. "The victory roar that greeted the announcement beat upon the eardrums until it numbed the senses," observed the *Times*.

Meanwhile, locals dressed in ritualistic dragon costumes led processions along Chinatown's narrow downtown streets as people crammed onto fire escapes, waved American and Chinese flags, and watched the sacred dance that symbolized peace. Across the East River in Queens, thousands staged impromptu parades, and in Bay Ridge, Brooklyn, residents strung up effigies of Japanese emperor Hirohito. Soldiers, sailors, and small boys first used them for target practice, and then set them ablaze. Similar celebrations broke out from Maine to California. And far to the west, in Honolulu, where the war began for America with the attack on Pearl Harbor on December 7, 1941, church bells pealed, military bands strutted, and families turned out in their Sunday best, while soldiers, sailors, Marines, and civilians hopped into jeeps and cars and cruised around the city, blaring their horns.

The most devastating war in human history was truly, indisputably over. It was almost impossible to believe. In Europe, where Nazi Germany had surrendered on May 7, troops who had nervously been preparing to take part in a planned invasion of Japan let out a collective sigh of joyous relief. Paul Fussell was a second lieutenant based near Rheims, France. Thirty-six years later the author recalled in an essay for the *New Republic* that "for all the practiced phlegm of our tough facades we broke down and cried... We were going to live. We were going to grow to adulthood after all."

Japan had begun the war in China by attacking Beijing in 1937; with Adolf Hitler's ravenous aggression in Europe two years later, bloodshed spread like a pandemic across the globe, taking the lives of 65 million people, including more than 400,000 American servicepeople. After years of grinding, seemingly interminable conflict, two U.S. attacks on Japanese cities with a terrifying new weapon hastened the war's end. The first use of the atomic bomb, on August 6, 1945, destroyed Hiroshima; the second, three days later, devastated Nagasaki. The twin mushroom clouds are believed to have killed almost 200,000 people and seemed to have been unleashed by an omnipotent, supernatural being, one whose wrathful power forced Hirohito—whom his people viewed as a descendant of the gods—to surrender.

Some 27,000 U.S. military members had been held prisoner by the emperor's forces. One of those now liberated was Lieutenant General Jonathan Wainwright, who had been imprisoned since the Philippines fell in 1942. Wainwright was the highest-ranking American POW, and following his release General Douglas MacArthur made sure he was on hand to take part in the official Victory Over Japan Day on September 2, 1945, as a witness to Japan's formal surrender onboard the USS *Missouri.*

While many states once celebrated that signing, now only Rhode Island remembers the occasion with its Victory Day. And of the 16 million Americans who served in the war, no more than 300,000 now survive. A dozen of those who fought at the Battle of Iwo Jima in 1945 returned to that speck of a volcanic island, now called Iwo To, in March 2019 to commemorate one of the Pacific war's bloodiest engagements, which took the lives of about 6,800 Americans and some 18,000 Japanese. Also at the ceremony were U.S. Marines and Japanese military troops. Yoshitaka Shindo, a member of Japan's House of Representatives and the grandson of Lieutenant General Tadamichi Kuribayashi, the battle's Japanese commander, also came to honor the fallen.

The once strapping and now bent American warriors all wondered why they were the lucky ones who could be there. "I had a lot of Marine buddies killed here," said E. Bruce Heilman, who served as a sergeant (and died at 93 in October 2019). "For 74 years these guys have been dead, and I've been having family and marriages and success. You think about that. Why me?" And Barney Leone, a former machinist's mate second class on the USS *Nemasket,* likewise remembered friends who headed off to their deaths, and how after the war he devoted his life to visiting schools to teach about the war and tell of the heroics of his comrades. "They died for each one of you," he said. "The freedom that you're enjoying, myself included, somebody paid for with their life. Appreciate the freedom you have, try to get along with each other. I'm 94 years of age now. I think I'm here to carry that mission out for those who are not able to be here to do that." ●

1

DAWN OF THE EMPIRE OF THE RISING SUN

1937–1941

JAPAN SOUGHT CONTROL OVER BOTH EASTERN ASIA AND A VAST STRETCH OF THE PACIFIC OCEAN AND BELIEVED IT NEEDED TO CRIPPLE THE UNITED STATES NAVY AT PEARL HARBOR TO PREVENT AMERICA'S INTERVENTION

SERVICEMEN ON FORD ISLAND in Pearl Harbor moments after the USS *Shaw* was hit during the second wave of the attack. The strikes caused the destroyer's ammunition magazines to explode.

ON THE EVENING OF JULY 7, 1937, JAPANESE soldiers took part in training exercises on the banks of China's Yongding River near Wanping's Marco Polo Bridge. The troops were there thanks to a 1901 treaty known as the Boxer Protocol, which allowed the Empire of Japan, along with several other countries, to keep a garrison in nearby Beijing to defend its diplomatic legation. On this summer night, the Japanese did more than merely drill by the riverside—they exchanged shots with Chinese troops. It's not clear who fired first, but Japan claimed one of its soldiers had gone missing and insisted on searching the city, returning to Wanping the next morning with armored vehicles. Things escalated from there: The Marco Polo Bridge Incident would ignite the Second Sino-Japanese War, considered by many to mark the beginning of World War II.

Japanese forces went on the offensive, taking Beijing and Tianjin by the end of July, then moved southward, conquering Shanghai in November. In December the capital at Nanjing fell. For six weeks troops burned and looted that city, and, on the orders of Commander Iwane Matsui, raped tens of thousands of women and casually slaughtered upwards of 300,000 people.

The Japanese had long dreamed of

JAPANESE TROOPS CELEBRATED their capture of Tienyuehssu, Manchuria, in March 1932. Their conquest of Asia had started with the attack on that Chinese province in 1931. Japan renamed it Manchukuo and installed Puyi, the last Chinese emperor, as its puppet ruler.

spreading their empire. By the start of the 20th century, the Land of the Rising Sun had transformed itself from a feudal state into an industrialized society. To grow, this island nation with limited agricultural lands and minerals needed coal, iron, and oil. To obtain such resources, Japan annexed Taiwan in 1895, Korea in 1910 and following World War I took over China's Shandong peninsula. With emperor Yoshihito's death in 1926, his son, the 25-year-old Hirohito, assumed the throne. To his people, he was descended from Amaterasu, the Shinto sun goddess. Deity or not, Hirohito had limited power, and could not control an inexorable build up of right-wing forces. In 1931 the Japanese army took over Manchuria in northeast China. And, just as in Adolf Hitler's Germany and Benito Mussolini's Italy, Japanese militarists vastly expanded their power.

By mid 1938, Japan controlled numerous Chinese provinces, parts of the coastline, and major cities. The grab was made possible because of the weak response of the Chinese, who were consumed with an internal power struggle between the Communists under Mao Zedong and the Nationalists under Chiang Kai-shek. While the foreign aggression brought about a fragile Chinese alliance, it could not stop Japan, which took over the southeastern province of Canton across from Hong Kong.

Believing itself surrounded by what were dubbed the ABCD powers—America, Britain, China, and the Dutch—Japan, under the sway of war minister General Hideki Tojo, sought even more territory. The war in Europe had begun in September 1939 with

CLOCKWISE FROM BOTTOM LEFT: Following the 1937 attack on the Marco Polo Bridge, Chinese troops headed to the front near Beijing. Shanghai's Zhabei district burned in the distance after a Japanese bombing raid in November 1937. A Japanese soldier prepared to execute a Chinese prisoner.

WHEN EMPEROR HIROHITO assumed the throne in 1926, he named his reign Showa, which means "enlightened harmony." Yet despite the trappings of peace, Japan would soon start its encroachment in China. Japanese Ambassador Saburo Kurusu, opposite, signed the Tripartite Pact, which called on Japan, Germany, and Italy to come to one another's defense in the event of an attack.

Hitler's attack on Poland, and the following September Japan struck an alliance with Germany and Italy. Their Tripartite Pact called on the signatories "to assist one another with all political, economic, and military means." Claiming to want "Asia for Asians," Japan rolled out the new Greater East Asia Co-Prosperity Sphere and set out to take over areas held by Western powers. This ostensible partnership for peace and economic welfare proved to be a ruse. In fact the Japanese coveted raw materials—oil in the Dutch East Indies; the rice paddies in French-controlled Indochina; rubber, tin, and other resources in British-ruled Malaya. Buoyed by its pact with Europe's Fascist leaders, Japan took over Indochina. In response, President Franklin Delano Roosevelt cut off Japanese access to oil, rubber, and steel. The British and the Dutch soon followed suit.

Now Japanese militarists were ready for an audacious next step: an attack on the United States to ensure that the Americans could not stop their conquest. A main proponent of that plan, Admiral Isoroku Yamamoto, believed that his forces needed to disable the U.S. fleet in Hawaii, calling it, "a dagger pointed at our throat." In January 1941 he ordered his staff to look into the idea of a surprise attack on the naval base at Pearl Harbor in Hawaii. Knowing Britain and the Netherlands were consumed with their war against the Nazis, Japan felt it could also easily seize the Dutch East Indies and Malaya.

ADMIRAL ISOROKU YAMAMOTO CALLED THE U.S. FLEET IN HAWAII "A DAGGER POINTED AT OUR THROAT."

To make all this possible, Yamamoto called for simultaneous attacks to take Thailand, Malaya, Singapore, Guam, Hong Kong, Wake Island, and the Philippines. To accomplish that, the empire needed stealth so its forces could move into position. Japanese envoys to Washington were tasked with negotiating an end to the embargo, a ploy to fool Americans into believing they were acting in good faith. Despite their efforts, hints emerged of unusual activities. As early as January 1941, the U.S. ambassador to Japan, Joseph Grew, had cabled the State Department about rumored Japanese plans for a surprise attack at Pearl Harbor. And, before the attack, American intelligence officers noticed the disappearance of Vice Admiral Chuichi Nagumo's fleet. Unfortunately, those and other warning signs went unheeded.

Nagumo's strike force set off for Hawaii on November 26. Led by six carriers, the *Akagi, Kaga, Soryu, Hiryu, Shokaku,* and *Zuikaku,* it included more than 420 planes, as well as battleships, cruisers, submarines, tankers, and destroyers. On the Hawaiian island of Oahu, people were blissfully unaware of the impending catastrophe. On December 6, Navy officers teed off at the Fort Shafter golf course. The University of Hawaii's football team tussled with Willamette University of Salem, Oregon. Twenty-one-year-old Ensign Charles J. Merdinger from the USS *Nevada* bought a small artificial tree, telling LIFE in 2001 that "it was going to brighten up our little cabin for Christmas." And sailors on shore leave visited taxi dance halls and watering holes like the Paradise Club and the Black Cat Café.

At four on the morning of the 7th, Lieutenant Kermit Tyler arrived at the U.S. Army's information center at Fort Shafter, about 30 miles south of the Opana radar station, where the men were just learning to use the equipment. Tyler wrote letters and read *Reader's Digest.* "It was quiet," he later recalled to LIFE. Meanwhile, military planes sat in rows in the open, and ships were grouped around Ford Island at the center of the harbor.

By then Nagumo's fleet had arrived 230 miles north of Oahu. In the early hours, Commander Mitsuo Fuchida entered the operation room in his flying togs. "I am ready for the mission," he told Nagumo, who grasped his hand and said, "I have confidence in you." The admiral planned a two-wave attack. The first, led by Fuchida, launched at six in the morning. He left with 89 B5N2 bombers—which the U.S. called "Kates"—brimming with both armor-piercing bombs and torpedoes. With them flew 51 Aichi D3A1 dive bombers, planes the Americans dubbed "Vals," along with 43 A6M Model 21 Zero fighters. At about 6:45 a.m. radar operators at Fort Shafter saw some blips on their screens and called the information center. There were no identification people on staff yet, and Tyler assumed a flight of B-17 bombers arriving from California caused the green dots on their displays. Ensign Victor Delano,

THE ARCHITECT AND THE administrators of the attack on Pearl Harbor, from top: Admiral Chuichi Nagumo orchestrated the plan; Admiral Isoroku Yamamoto devised the assault; and Commander Mitsuo Fuchida led the first wave. Opposite: Japanese crewmen cheered, top, as their planes set out for Hawaii; Pearl Harbor moments after the start of the attack.

a distant relative of the President, was onboard the USS *West Virginia* reading *The New Yorker* over a breakfast of pineapples and waffles. Ensign Merdinger on the *Nevada* prepared to attend mass. High schooler Ronald Oba enjoyed hot cakes with his family, while 17-year-old Daniel Inouye was readying for church.

At 7:49 Fuchida spotted Pearl Harbor and gave the command to set off the assault, *"To-ra, to-ra, to-ra,"* ("Tiger, tiger, tiger.") As the brass band on the *Nevada* raised the flag and played "The Star Spangled Banner," Japanese pilots swooped toward Wheeler and Hickam Fields, knocked out the parked planes, and released torpedoes toward the ships. "I heard shouting through an overhead grating that there was an attack," Delano told LIFE in 2001. "I went from there to my battle station." Troops manned machine guns and fired at Fuchida's marauders. "As my group made its bomb run, enemy antiaircraft suddenly came to life," Fuchida recalled. "Dark gray bursts blossomed here and there until the sky was clouded with shattering near misses that made our plane tremble."

Some American shells hit Fuchida's plane—"It was not easy to pass through the concentrated antiaircraft fire," he wrote later—but he continued the mission, and thrilled as his men dove for the anchored ships, hitting the USS *Raleigh, Helena, Utah, California,* and *Oklahoma.* "This boy just slumped over. Blood was all over everything," *Oklahoma* seaman Garlen Eslick said of a wounded comrade.

Right after that came two explosions on the USS *Arizona,* and then at

8:10 a.m. a 1,763-pound bomb slammed into that ship, igniting more than a million pounds of gunpowder. The blast engulfed the *Arizona,* causing its front upper portion to collapse into the hull, killing 1,177 men. Others from Fuchida's fleet struck the *West Virginia.* "The torpedoes came in the side and demolished the whole side of the ship," Delano recalled. "The torpedoes ruptured the tanks and the oil was mixed with the water. Water and a lot of oil had begun to work its way through watertight doors." Two torpedoes holed the *Utah,* which started to capsize. As water and oil filled the ships, fires raged. Below decks, the lights began to dim and go out. "With all these fumes and stuff, my eyes were burning," said Seaman Eslick. "I had saltwater, gasoline, bunker oil, and stuff all in my eyes."

By 8:35 the first wave had ended. But then at 8:54 the second assault,

"THE TORPEDOES CAME IN ... AND DEMOLISHED THE WHOLE SIDE OF THE SHIP," DELANO RECALLED.

under the command of Lieutenant Commander Shigekazu Shimazaki, arrived with 167 planes, including 54 high-level bombers and 78 dive bombers. They struck the Navy yard dry dock and the battleship *Pennsylvania,* the destroyers *Cassin* and *Downes,* and the light cruiser *Raleigh.* With fires blazing on the neighboring *Arizona,* Lieutenant Commander Francis Thomas tried to save his ship. He counterflooded the *Nevada* and got it underway. But when the Japanese saw the vessel heading toward the sea, they hit it with five dive-bombs, sending water rushing in and setting the ship ablaze. Thomas then ran the *Nevada* aground so it wouldn't sink; tugs then moved it clear of the shipping lane.

Delano managed to bring some of his men topside. There they found the

CONTINUED ON PAGE 21

THE USS *SHAW* WAS IN DRY dock for repairs when Japanese bombs struck it during the second wave. The fires could not be extinguished, and the destroyer was ordered abandoned. As crews tried to flood the dry dock, the vessel's ammunition magazine exploded. Despite the damage, the *Shaw* would be fitted with a new bow and put back into action.

A SAILOR SOUGHT COVER AT Kaneohe Bay, top, as a crew extinguished a burning plane. The USS *West Virginia*, right, was struck by some nine torpedoes, which tore open its midships and forward hull. The vessel was moored on Battleship Row alongside the USS *Tennessee*, which was hit by two bombs and can be seen behind it. The *Tennessee* was set afire by burning debris when the USS *Arizona* exploded. Sailors at Kaneohe Bay tried to beach a PBY Catalina flying boat that was hit, above. A later strike destroyed the seaplane.

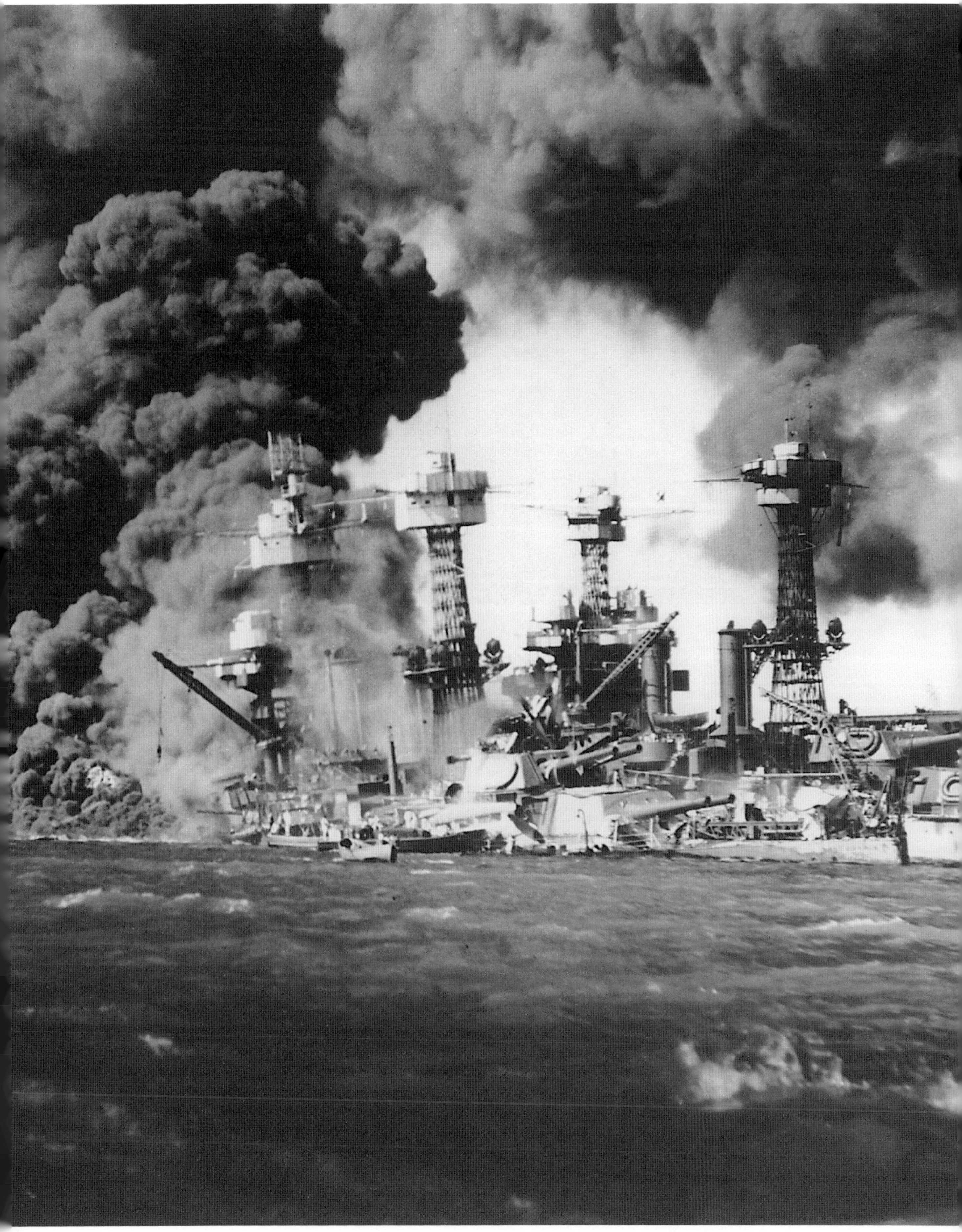

CONTINUED FROM PAGE 16

command tower destroyed and Captain Mervyn S. Bennion gravely wounded by shrapnel. The captain refused to leave his post to be taken to a first aid station, so Delano found some ether to numb his pain. Delano then got two of the *West Virginia*'s .50 caliber water-cooled machine guns going, but the men had to stop using them when they overheated and jammed because of a lack of water. By then, smoke had engulfed everyone on deck. Choking from the fumes—"paint burns, oil burns, and other flammable materials burn"—the ensign soon had no other choice but to plunge into the harbor. "Just as I started, fire broke out on the water ahead of me," he said, referring to the burning oil slicks. "I was just trying to keep away from whatever oil I could keep away from." He soon made it ashore to Ford Island, where he joined with others and headed back to his ship with gas masks and fire hoses. But once he was on board, there was an explosion, and the next thing Delano recalled was being on a boat heading toward the submarine-base hospital.

All over, rescue workers rushed men to the hospital. "Amputees. They started coming in and they had arms and legs just shot off—a terrible mass of tissues, bones, blood," recalled Lieutenant Elizabeth Murphy. Schools, barracks, and assorted buildings were turned into makeshift medical units. Inouye, who dreamed of becoming a surgeon, was a Red Cross volunteer and raced to the Lunalilo School, where he treated wounded civilians and tended to bodies in an improvised morgue.

The second wave ended at around 10 a.m. Throughout the base, men were trapped in their ships. "We stayed in that compartment rapping out this SOS," said Eslick. "I don't know how long it was. We could hear the boys, some of them, in this one compartment next to us, and they were hollering for help for a good long time. There wasn't anything we could do about it, and then they became quiet. They evidently drowned." Merdinger and his men spent seven hours trapped below the *Nevada*'s deck. When they finally emerged, he recalled, "I looked around—the whole world was on fire."

A BOAT RESCUED CREW FROM the *West Virginia*, left. The masts of the *Tennessee* can be seen in the background. Wounded civilians were treated at an outdoor aid station at a high school, while soldiers on the roof extinguished fires, above.

NEW YORKERS LEARNED about the attack at one of the city's newsreel theaters, above. The day after Pearl Harbor, President Franklin Delano Roosevelt called on Congress to declare war on Japan. The Senate voted 82 to 0 in favor; the House vote was 388 to 1. (The lone dissenter was pacifist congresswoman Jeannette Rankin, Republican of Montana.)

Of 1,500 aboard Merdinger's ship, about 50 died. The *West Virginia* lost more than 100, including Captain Bennion. On the *Arizona* 1,102 of the 1,177 killed became entombed in the hull. All told, the Japanese killed 2,008 members of the Navy, 109 Marines, 218 Army soldiers, and 68 civilians; 188 planes were destroyed and more than 150 others damaged; at least 18 ships were destroyed or damaged. Oba told LIFE that when ships unloaded bodies, they "were piled high like cords."

The Japanese, meanwhile, lost just 29 planes, 55 airmen, and nine midget-sub crewmen. Like the Nazi blitzkrieg attack on Poland on September 1, 1939, which started the war in Europe, the assault on Oahu proved overwhelming. And even though Fuchida felt they should have launched a third wave, Nagumo decided not to order one. Fortunately, America's Pacific fleet carriers, the USS *Enterprise, Lexington,* and *Saratoga,* had been away at sea, and the naval dockyards and oil facilities as well as the submarine pens escaped destruction, albeit with some damage.

British prime minister Winston Churchill called Roosevelt to find out what had happened. The President confirmed the worst: "It's quite true. They have attacked us at Pearl Harbor. We are all in the same boat now." On December 8, FDR appeared before a joint session of Congress and called the previous day "a date which will live in infamy." Congress then declared war. Hitler was ecstatic, proclaiming, "We can't lose . . . We now have an ally which has never been conquered in 3,000 years." Taking a more tempered view was none other than Admiral Yamamoto, who had argued for years against attacking the United States. He had worked as a naval attaché in Washington in the 1920s and understood America's industrial strength. "For a while we'll have everything our own way, stretching out in every direction like an octopus spreading its tentacles," Yamamoto said in September 1941. "But it'll last for a year and a half at the most." ●

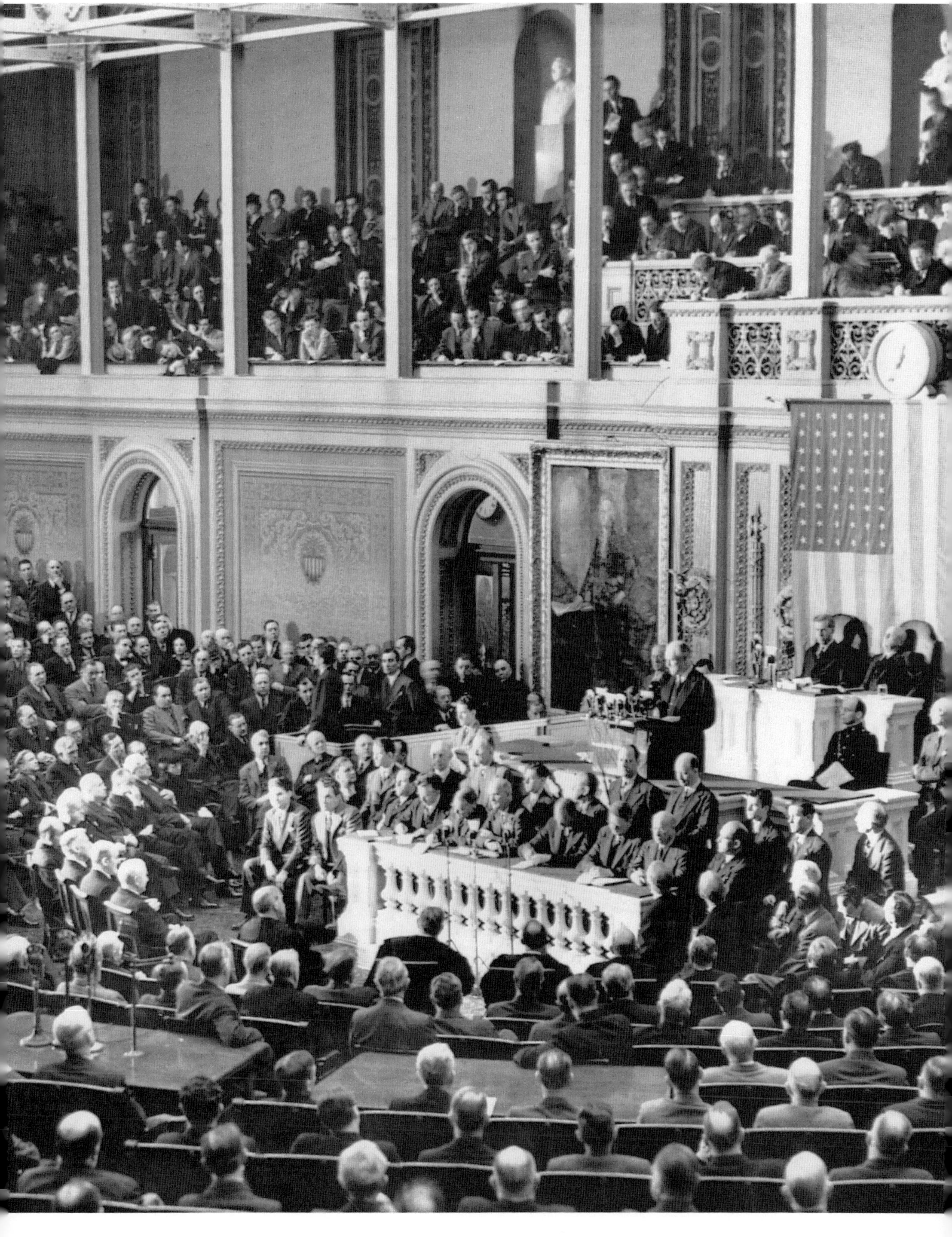

FIVE MONTHS AFTER THE United States entered World War II, sailors at Pearl Harbor observed an ancient Hawaiian tradition and draped leis on the graves of their comrades killed on December 7, 1941.

MARINES TOOK A BEACH IN Guadalcanal in August 1942 at the beginning of the battle to wrest the Solomon Islands from the Japanese. The fight would last six full months.

2

CONQUERING ISLANDS TO TURN THE TIDE

1942–1943

AFTER JAPAN CAPTURED A SPRAWLING AREA, AMERICA AND ITS ALLIES MADE A SLOW ADVANCE, BATTLING FORCES ON SUCH ISLANDS AS GUADALCANAL, NEW GUINEA, AND TARAWA

T

THE JAPANESE ATTACKED FAR MORE than Pearl Harbor. At the same time, they set off months of invasions, targeting Thailand, Guam, Wake Island, Hong Kong, and Malaya. Their forces sieged Singapore, cut off its water supply, and forced British Lieutenant General Arthur Percival to surrender to General Tomoyuki Yamashita on February 15, 1942. They attacked Burma to the west, while in the east capturing the Dutch East Indies islands of Sulawesi, Bali, Timor, Java, Borneo, and parts of New Guinea.

When the Japanese bombed Hawaii, General Douglas MacArthur was awakened with the news. Commander of U.S. Army forces in the Far East, the brilliant and imperious World War I hero was based in the Philippines and realized Japan also coveted that semi-independent commonwealth. Japanese pilots flying toward the main Philippine island of Luzon on December 8, 1941, found American planes neatly lined up on the ground, just as they'd been at Pearl Harbor. They destroyed half of them—about 100 aircraft—and invaded Manila. MacArthur's troops fought back and, with supplies and ammunition dwindling, retreated in late December to

AMERICAN TROOPS IN APRIL 1942 at the start of the Bataan Death March, during which the Japanese brutalized and beheaded prisoners, even burying some of them alive.

the jungle-clad Bataan Peninsula on Manila Bay, as well as to the rocky Corregidor Island to its south.

Conditions there proved dire. Low on food and enduring relentless Japanese bombings, American and Filipino troops took to eating horses and even monkeys. Diseases from dysentery to scurvy sapped their strength, while dozens of nurses—dubbed the Angels of Bataan and Corregidor—tended their battle wounds. As Army sergeant Lester Tenney recalled, "Our food was gone, our health was deteriorating, and our ammunition and gas had just about run out." Not wanting to lose one of his illustrious commanders, President Roosevelt ordered MacArthur to personally evacuate. When the general landed in Australia he vowed, "I shall return."

Lieutenant General Jonathan "Skinny" Wainwright took charge of MacArthur's men but could not withstand the unrelenting assaults.

"OUR FOOD WAS GONE, OUR HEALTH WAS DETERIORATING, AND OUR AMMUNITION AND GAS HAD JUST ABOUT RUN OUT."

Allied forces on Bataan surrendered on April 9; in the interest of averting slaughter, Wainwright yielded Corregidor on May 6. The Japanese then forced their 76,000 American and Filipino POWs through the jungle to a prison 66 miles away, beating them along the way. "A fierce jab with a bayonet into the chest or a bullet in the head was administered with dispatch and the body was pushed into a ditch or the bushes," recalled Captain John Olson. Only 54,000 survived what became known as the Bataan Death March. The nurses were meanwhile placed in an internment camp on the campus of Santo Tomás University in Manila. There Mildred Manning and her colleagues tended to 4,000 incarcerated men, women, and children. "We were under terrific strain," she said, "but we just did our job, even when we were weak from not eating."

The coordinated Japanese assaults succeeded. In no time the flag of the Rising Sun flew over an area that ranged from India to the central Pacific and the waters above Australia up toward the Aleutian Islands. Japan believed it had created a massive buffer that would keep its enemies at bay. Like the Nazis, the Japanese viewed those they had conquered as inferior beings, dismissing their Western captives as apish brutes. And despite all those grand claims of a Greater East Asia Co-Prosperity Sphere, they turned their new Asian subjects into slaves. In Singapore, the Japanese began their *Sook Ching* (purge through cleansing)

CAPTURED AMERICAN servicemen emerging from Corregidor's Malinta Tunnel in May 1942, opposite. Here, Japanese troops lowered the Stars and Stripes.

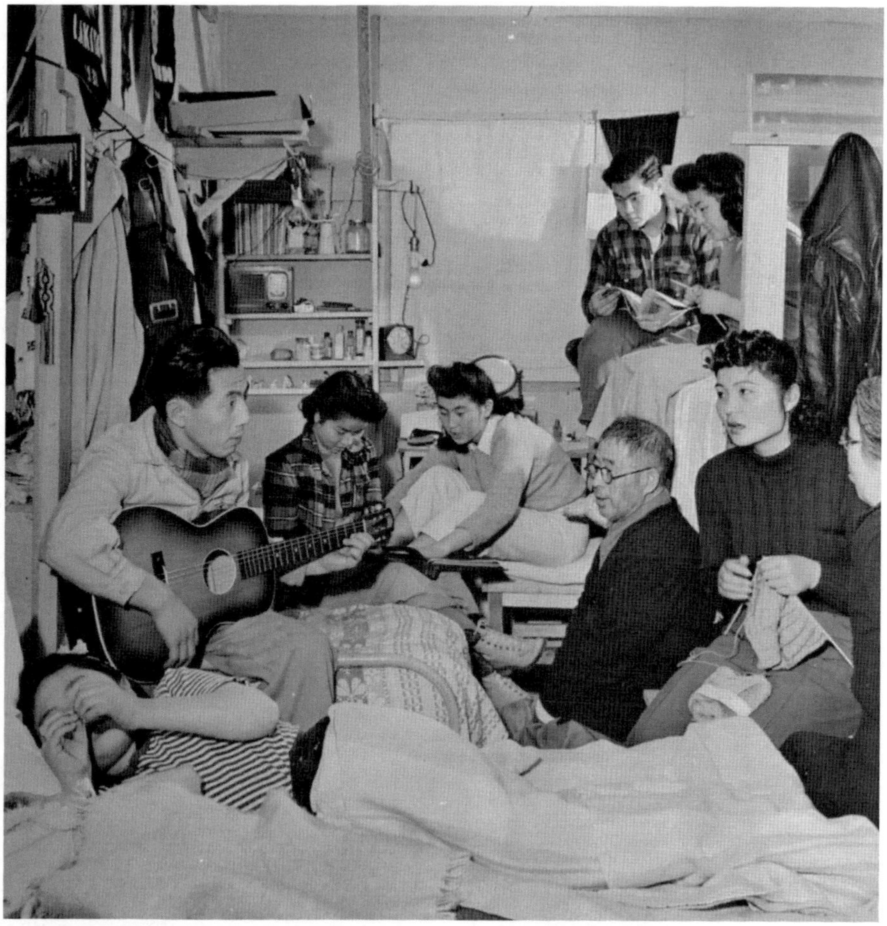

massacres, slaughtering thousands of Chinese they believed hostile to the emperor. Two hundred thousand women and girls—Korean, Chinese, Indonesian, and Dutch, among other nationalities—were taken prisoner and systematically abused by the military as sexual slaves.

But instead of cowing the West, the attacks only steeled the Allies' resolve. American enlistment centers became overwhelmed with recruits. James Young left his work at a Pennsylvania shoe factory, hitchhiked to Philadelphia, and signed up as a Marine. Desmond Doss, a Seventh-Day Adventist who refused to bear arms, enlisted as a medic. George Herbert Walker Bush entered the Navy. E. Bruce Heilman dropped out of high school in Kentucky and joined the Marines.

Acting out of race-based fear, the government unjustly rounded up Japanese immigrants and U.S. citizens of Japanese descent and incarcerated more than 100,000 of them in internment camps. Despite their mistreatment, some 33,000 signed up for the military. Ronald Oba and Daniel Inouye, who had both watched the destruction at Pearl Harbor, joined the 442nd Regimental Combat Team, composed almost entirely of second-generation Japanese Americans. As Oba left, his parents told him, "You don't bring shame to the family. You fight and die in the front lines." Women and African Americans also enlisted in droves. Eventually 16 million Americans served in what had become a world war spanning Europe, Africa, Asia, and the Pacific Ocean.

In February 1942, the newly created Joint Chiefs of Staff and their British counterparts split the Pacific into two

JAPANESE AMERICANS WERE viewed as a danger and forced into camps such as the Heart Mountain Relocation Center in Wyoming, left and above. The crowded barracks housed 10,767 internees, making it that state's third largest community.

CONTINUED ON PAGE 36

AS THE NATION GEARED UP for war, citizens, like these 18-year-olds, top, signed up in droves. The women above assembled the fuselage of a plane at the Lockheed plant in Burbank, California. During the war the United States produced 300,000 planes; the Japanese produced 67,000. Shipbuilders laid the keel for the *Joseph B. Teal,* right, a 10,500-ton Liberty freighter, which they completed in a record 10 days.

LIEUTENANT COLONEL JAMES Doolittle, left, inspected a bomb on the deck of the USS *Hornet* before the start of his April 18, 1942, raid on Tokyo. Here, one of the Doolittle Raiders' B-25 bombers took off from the carrier's deck.

CONTINUED FROM PAGE 33

theaters of war. MacArthur was made supreme commander of the Southwest Pacific Area—which included the Dutch East Indies, the Philippines, Australia, the Solomon Islands, and the Bismarck Archipelago—while Admiral Chester W. Nimitz oversaw the Pacific Ocean Areas.

With a war on multiple fronts, new ships, planes, tanks, guns, and other matériel were needed. The government sought to turn peacetime industries into what Roosevelt, in a December 1940 "fireside chat," had called the "Arsenal of Democracy." Unimpressed, German Reichsmarschall Hermann Göring scoffed that the Americans could only produce refrigerators and razor blades, and not the weaponry needed to defeat the Axis powers.

In fact, the Axis had awakened a sleeping giant. The ramping-up of production in this land of 133 million people put post-Depression America to work. Industries—the ones that produced those fridges and sharp blades, among myriad other items—were transformed. Roosevelt recruited business leaders such as General Motors president William Knudsen to crank out guns, jeeps, tanks, ships, antiaircraft guns, and aircraft. Small factories geared up, too. To staff the

THE AXIS HAD AWAKENED A SLEEPING GIANT. THE RAMPING-UP OF PRODUCTION PUT POST-DEPRESSION AMERICA TO WORK.

assembly lines, women entered the workforce. African Americans had long been excluded from such labor, but Roosevelt issued an executive order banning racial discrimination in federally contracted defense industries.

The entertainment industry likewise swung into action, and Hollywood turned out movies to instill patriotic fervor. There were many about the Pacific war. In 1942, Anna May Wong starred in *Lady from Chungking,* about Chinese guerillas fighting the Japanese. Robert Taylor appeared in 1943's *Bataan,* about the attack in the Philippines. Even Donald Duck joined up and single-handedly destroyed a Japanese jungle air base in 1944's *Commando Duck.*

A war of such unprecedented scope, with so much at stake, required new types of weaponry. Knowing the Nazis were seeking a way to use nuclear

JAPANESE PILOTS FROM THE carrier *Hiryu* attacked the USS *Yorktown* on June 4, 1942, during the pivotal Battle of Midway. The Japanese submarine *I-168* torpedoed the crippled carrier on June 6 and it sank the next day. The ship's wreck was discovered in 1998 by Robert Ballard, who also found the *Titanic*. Right: The deck of the USS *Enterprise*, which became the most decorated vessel of World War II.

fission to make a bomb, American scientists started looking into the idea in 1939. That year Nobel laureate physicist Albert Einstein wrote to Roosevelt about the possibility of building such a device. Scientists were then recruited and labs and facilities set up. Early work began at New York's Columbia University, and the program, which became known as the Manhattan Project, soon had outposts across the country, including a secret city that physicist J. Robert Oppenheimer set up in Los Alamos, New Mexico.

Still battered by the devastating losses at Pearl Harbor, the United States resolved to prove it was a force to be reckoned with. On April 18, Lieutenant Colonel James Doolittle took the lead, and brought 16 B-25 bombers to the heart of the enemy's empire. Though they inflicted little damage, the bombing raids on Tokyo and four other Japanese cities thrilled Americans, none more than the U.S. diplomatic staff held prisoner in the Japanese capital, who climbed excitedly to the embassy's roof as they heard the approaching planes.

Despite this Allied morale booster, the Japanese onslaught continued. They took Bougainville, the Admiralty Islands, and New Britain, where

ADMIRAL YAMAMOTO SAW MIDWAY ISLAND AS AN IDEAL BASE FROM WHICH TO LAUNCH FURTHER STRIKES ON HAWAII.

Australian naval and air facilities at Rabaul afforded them an ideal base from which to launch attacks. Seeking to isolate Australia, they set out to take control of Fiji and Samoa, as well as to set up bases in Port Moresby in southeastern Papua New Guinea. In order to succeed, they needed control of the Coral Sea between eastern Australia and the French island of New Caledonia. The U.S. Navy, though, had already cracked Japan's main naval code, and was aware of their plans. The Americans confronted the Japanese and their fleets in early May. With their ships 175 miles apart, the two forces waged the world's first all-carrier battle, with planes doing all the fighting. And though the Japanese tactically won the Battle of the Coral Sea, the Allies stopped their attack on Port Moresby—the first time Japan was prevented from reaching an objective in the Pacific.

To further consolidate the Japanese position, Admiral Isoroku Yamamoto hoped to capture Midway Island. He saw the tiny atoll as an ideal base from which to launch further strikes at Hawaii, and dispatched much of his fleet there, including four light aircraft carriers, two seaplane carriers, seven battleships, 15 cruisers, 42 destroyers, and 10 submarines, along with support and escort vessels. But American code breakers discovered Yamamoto's plan. In response, Nimitz sent the carriers *Enterprise, Hornet,* and *Yorktown,* along with cruisers, destroyers, and subs, as well as Army, Navy, and Marine aircraft. Undetected, his armada waited out of range of Admiral Chuichi Nagumo's observation planes.

Mitsuo Fuchida was supposed to lead the new assault, but an appendectomy sidelined the captain who six months earlier had led the attack on Pearl Harbor. He therefore could only observe the preparations from the *Akagi's* bridge and cheer on his comrades as they took off for Midway on June 4. As their planes approached the island, the Americans quickly responded with 41 Douglas TBD-1 Devastators, but Japanese fighters intercepted the torpedo bombers and shot down all but six of them. American dive bombers from the *Enterprise, Hornet,* and *Yorktown* then arrived and in five minutes delivered a devastating blow. Lieutenant Clarence Dickinson swooped down on the *Kaga,* and later recalled, "I saw the 500-pound bomb hit right abreast of the island [command tower]. The two 100-bombs struck in the forward area of the parked planes on that yellow flight deck."

As the *Kaga* sank, other American planes appeared, and a horrified Fuchida watched them set upon the *Akagi*: "Bombs! Down they came straight towards me! I fell intuitively to the deck and crawled behind a command post mantelet." Fire consumed his ship. During the attack Fuchida broke both his ankles, and he had to be carried off to a rescue boat. The *Akagi* then sank. A submarine destroyed the *Soryu,* taking the lives of 718 sailors.

THESE SOLDIERS, ABOVE, partly buried in the tidal sands of Guadalcanal's Tenaru River, were a few of the 24,000 Japanese troops to die during the Battle of Guadalcanal. Right: Battle-weary Marines waited to be taken off the island.

The *Hiryu* launched a counterattack and struck the *Yorktown,* causing it to be abandoned. But American planes then destroyed the *Hiryu,* which "was hit and hit again with bombs timed to pierce her deck till she burned from end to end," reported the *New York Post.* The crippled Japanese fleet withdrew, and Nimitz deemed Midway "the most crucial battle of the Pacific War, the engagement that made everything possible."

Now on the offensive, U.S. forces began hopping from island to island, conquering territory as they went. Since Japanese air bases on islands east of New Guinea, such as Guadalcanal, could be used to threaten American ships heading to Australia and New Zealand, Marines stormed Guadalcanal, along with Tulagi, Florida, and other islands, on August 7 in Operation Watchtower. But the Japanese were not dislodged, and they dispatched reinforcements in an effort to hold on to the island. Deadly battles broke out at places like the one on Guadalcanal Americans dubbed Bloody Ridge. "The Japanese attack was almost constant, like a rain that subsides for a moment and then pours the harder," recalled Captain William McKennan. "When one wave was mowed down—and I mean mowed down—another followed it into death." By mid October the Japanese had 22,000 troops up against 23,000 Marines. As they continued to reinforce their sides, many succumbed to malaria and other tropical diseases. Yet the Americans slowly widened their hold, and by February the Japanese withdrew, having lost 24,000 men.

As this was going on, the Japanese were trying again to take Port Moresby. They had landed troops at Buna on New Guinea's east coast the previous July and started hiking to Moresby via the Kokoda Track. The path took them over the steep Owen Stanley Range, the long tail of land on the island's eastern edge. They also put troops ashore at Milne Bay at the far tip. But while making the arduous trek, they fell prey to Australian and American forces and to illness. By January the Japanese, having lost 12,000 men, pulled out.

There were also smaller attacks and surveillance. The Japanese navy ran what the Americans called the "Tokyo Express," nightly deliveries of supplies and men to Guadalcanal through a channel between the islands

LIFE MAGAZINE'S 1943 photograph of three American bodies on New Guinea's Buna Beach, opposite, was the first time an image of dead servicemen appeared in an American publication during World War II. Above: New Guinean tribesmen helped a wounded Allied soldier.

that Americans dubbed "the Slot." U.S. Patrol Torpedo (PT) boats regularly skimmed those waters, seeking to damage convoys. On August 1, 1943, 15 PT boats set out on the Blackett Strait. They failed to disrupt the enemy and started to head back to base. But at 2:30 a.m. the *Amagiri* appeared off *PT 109*'s starboard bow. The Japanese destroyer split the boat in half, throwing most of the men into the water. Lieutenant John F. Kennedy gathered those still alive, and the following morning they swam three and a half miles to an islet called Plum Pudding Island, with Kennedy towing one of his injured men with a belt clamped between his teeth. He left his crew there and swam to other islands in search of aid. Finally convincing locals to help him, JFK carved a message on a coconut, and the Navy rescued the sailors on the 8th.

In March the Japanese lost the Battle of the Bismarck Sea to the Australians and the Americans. Then in April, Yamamoto flew to Rabaul on New Britain. The Americans learned of his plan to inspect his troops at Bougainville on the 18th, and Pacific Fleet commander William "Bull" Halsey Jr. cabled, TALLY HO X LET'S GET THE BASTARD. Operation Vengeance dispatched at least 16 Lockheed P-38G Lightnings. The pilots flew low so as not to be picked up on radar and after two and a half hours came upon six Zeros escorting Yamamoto's two Mitsubishi bombers. While most of the fighters focused on the Zeros, Lieutenant Rex T. Barber, Captain Thomas G. Lanphier Jr., and two other pilots targeted the bomber. "I started shooting across the tail into the right engine," recalled Barber. "Pieces of the cowling flew up and hit me." The admiral's plane crashed on Bougainville, and after Japanese rescue workers found the wreckage, his ashes were returned to Japan for a state funeral.

By then, it wasn't only in the Pacific where the Allies were advancing. On the other side of the world, American and British troops, as part of Operation Torch, invaded North Africa in late 1942 and prepared for an invasion of southern Europe. And the Russians in 1943 prevented the capture of Stalingrad and stopped Germany's advance into the Soviet Union.

On the home front, by mid 1943 the United States was in high gear turning out weaponry and troops. Meanwhile, it was increasingly apparent to the Americans that they needed

FROM THE USS *MARYLAND*, Rear Admiral Harry Hill led the amphibious assault group that wrested the fortress of Tarawa from Japanese rear admiral Keiji Shibazaki.

After being awarded the Presidential Medal of Freedom in 1951, Claire Phillips was greeted by Major Kenneth Boggs and a Women's Army Corps honor guard at New York's La Guardia Airport.

CASABLANCA EAST

At her Manila nightclub, Claire Phillips charmed intel out of Japanese officers and smuggled it to American and Filipino guerillas in the jungle

MANILA'S TSUBAKI CLUB offered guests cool drinks, torch songs, and alluring women. Most of all, Japanese officers and businessmen visiting the night spot on Manila Bay enjoyed the attentions of Dorothy Fuentes, the curvy Filipina-Italian hostess with the high-slit gown. Little did they know Fuentes was really Claire Phillips, a singer turned Allied spy from Portland, Oregon. The widow of Sergeant John Phillips, who survived the Bataan Death March but died in Cabanatuan prison camp in July 1942, she opened the Tsubaki Club that fall—naming it for the Japanese camellia flower—and used it as the base for her espionage ring.

At the nightclub's small cocktail tables, the audience took in the show, and happily listened to such popular prewar American standards as "I Don't Want to Set the World on Fire." While Phillips and others sang, her charming young staff acted like geishas, ordered rounds of expensive liquor for the officers, and coyly asked them about their lives, all the while gleaning military intel. The following morning Phillips—who went by the code name High-Pockets because she carried information in her bra—would compile a list of officers, units, even ships, and slip it to resistance guerillas. She likewise arranged for food and medicine to be taken to the prisoners held at Santo Tomás University.

Phillips and company did all this while feigning support for Japan and regularly toasting "death to Americans." (As she noted in her diary, she had to "drink to [the] downfall of England and America with finger crossed.") Throughout, Phillips endured physical abuse at the hands of the Japanese, and also lived in fear of being mistaken by the locals as a collaborator. Then in May 1944, the Gestapo-like Kempeitai clapped her into Manila's Bilibid Prison. There her captors waterboarded Phillips, carried out a mock beheading, and sentenced her to death, which was commuted to hard labor.

Freed in February 1945, Phillips returned Stateside in April. She wrote a memoir, which was made into the 1951 film *I Was an American Spy*. At General Douglas MacArthur's urging, Phillips received the Presidential Medal of Freedom. Her health weakened by post-traumatic stress disorder, she died of meningitis at age 52 in 1960.

to invade Japan. And so, they set off Operation Cartwheel. The plan was for MacArthur to capture northeastern New Guinea as Nimitz's forces advanced through the Solomon Islands toward the central Pacific. Nimitz's offensive began in November, landing on the Gilbert Islands, a series of coral islands and atolls along the equator. Bracing for an attack, Rear Admiral Keiji Shibazaki declared, "It would take one million men 100 years" to capture the Tarawa atoll, and had his men build bunkers, plant mines, and position artillery. They "used stone-hard coconut logs, steel rails, concrete, and sand to make incredibly stout fortifications," reported *Time's* Robert Sherrod.

Despite the boast, Rear Admiral Howard Kingman was not deterred.

"IT WOULD TAKE ONE MILLION MEN 100 YEARS" TO CAPTURE TARAWA, SAID ADMIRAL SHIBAZAKI.

The Marines headed to the islet of Betio on November 20. But because of heavy fire they had to land in the water and wade over the coral. "Those who were not hit would always remember how the bullets hissed into the water inches to the right, inches to the left," wrote Sherrod. The next day the Americans brought in tanks and artillery. Once off the beach they stormed Shibazaki's barricades. And instead of 100 years, the Marines mopped up in 76 hours of fierce fighting. By then the *New York Times* reported that "the dead of both sides lie all over the island, and riddled corpses form a ghastly fringe along the narrow white beaches where men of the Second Marine Division died for every foot of sand."

Of the 4,836 Japanese on the atoll, only 17 did not fight to the death. It was an ominous sign of what America could expect. ●

MARINES CLIMBING OVER A coconut-log seawall, part of the elaborate fortress system constructed by Japanese troops on the island of Tarawa.

3

I SHALL DIE FOR THE EMPEROR

1944

TO TAKE THE PACIFIC, U.S. FORCES STORMED REMOTE ISLANDS TRANSFORMED BY THE JAPANESE MILITARY INTO FORTRESSES WHERE TROOPS FORCED LOCALS TO CHOOSE SUICIDE OVER SURRENDER AND COMMANDERS DISPATCHED KAMIKAZE PILOTS WHO SLAMMED THEIR PLANES INTO ALLIED SHIPS

A JAPANESE FIGHTER PLANE plunged toward the sea on June 18, 1944, after being struck by U.S. forces during an aerial battle near the Northern Mariana Islands.

B

BY MID 1944, THE ALLIES CONTROLLED THE Solomon, Marshall, and Gilbert Islands in the western Pacific, and American submarines were having a field day sinking Japanese troop ships and warships and severing their maritime supply lines. As Commander Thomas Jeter had proclaimed two years earlier:

An eye for an eye,
A tooth for a tooth,
This Sunday, it's our turn to shoot.
Remember Pearl Harbor.

The Japanese still held the Mariana Islands, the Philippines, the Caroline Islands, and others. Yet their heavily fortified base on Rabaul in New Britain had been isolated and thus neutralized—so, in General Douglas MacArthur's words, it should just "wither on the vine." And then on March 31, Admiral Mineichi Koga, who succeeded Admiral Isoroku Yamamoto as commander-in-chief of the Imperial Japanese fleet, died when his plane crashed during a typhoon.

In order to secure air bases from which they could easily bomb Tokyo, the Joint Chiefs targeted Guam, Saipan, and Tinian in the Mariana Islands, 1,500 miles east of the Philippines. Taking those islands would also further cut off the Japanese's access to resources. Operation Forager began on June 15, scarcely more than a week after the Allies stormed the beaches of Normandy. The Japanese braced for the assault.

Destroyers and planes bombed Saipan in preparation for the invasion. Troops under the command of Marine general Holland "Howlin' Mad" Smith headed out with amphibious tanks and landing craft and stormed eight beaches. The shelling, though, did not take out many of the Japanese gun emplacements, which had been dug into the cliffs overlooking the water. The Japanese had also set flags in the surf so they could more easily target the Americans. "I could see the bullets striking the water right in front of us," recalled Colonel James Donovan. "I told the men to get down as low as they could. Next thing, my lieutenant was hit in his left shoulder. He looked down to his shoulder and his left eye was shot out. The man standing next to me had his head knocked off by an anti-tank."

Things did not improve once the men hit the beach, where they crouched for cover in the sand. The nightmarish landing continued into the dark, with the Americans sustaining 3,500 casualties in the first 24 hours. "We had no place to go. We had no foxholes," recalled rifle platoon leader John S. Chapin. "All around us was the chaotic debris of . . . combat—Jap and Marine bodies lying in mangled and grotesque positions, blasted and burnt-out pillboxes, burning wrecks of LVTs that had been knocked out by Jap high-velocity fire, the acrid smell of high explosives, the shattered trees, and the churned-up sand littered with discarded equipment." But soon 20,000 Marines and other combat-ready fighters established a beachhead,

A MARINE, HIS FACE GRIMY with coral dust, on the beach of Eniwetok, an atoll in the Marshall Islands, opposite. The invasion, commanded by Rear Admiral Harry Hill, with the Marines led by Colonel John Walker, was called Operation Catchpole.

joined in short order by Army troops.

Learning of the attack, the Japanese dispatched a fleet toward the Marianas under the command of Admiral Jisaburo Ozawa. Ozawa's destroyers, battleships, cruisers, and some 440 planes met up with Admiral Raymond Spruance's Fifth Fleet and its 905 fighters, dive bombers, and torpedo planes. In what became known as the Battle of the Philippine Sea, the Japanese launched waves of attacks. Many of their pilots were green, though, with just three months of training, and their planes lacked sufficient armor and self-sealing fuel tanks.

The American pilots, on the other hand, had two years of experience under their belts, and during the engagement, which has earned the nickname the Great Marianas Turkey Shoot, they shot down more than 300 planes on the first day—Lieutenant Alexander Vraciu scored six in just eight minutes—while losing only about 29. And the submarine *Albacore* targeted Ozawa's flagship carrier, the *Taiho* ("Great Phoenix"), causing a cascade of explosions and taking it to the bottom with 1,650 men. The carrier *Shokaku,* which took part in the attack on Pearl Harbor, likewise sank with 1,272 men.

MARINES TOOK THEIR POSITION on a Saipan beach, left, as one of their amphibious tractors used for the landing burned in the background after being struck by Japanese artillery. Above: A Marine tended to a comrade wounded during the fighting.

Helpless to prevent the Americans from advancing on Saipan, Lieutenant General Yoshitsugu Saito's forces sought shelter at Mount Tapochau a 1,550-foot peak at the center of the island. There the Americans encountered a rugged terrain and brutal battles, bestowing on areas such names as Death Valley and Purple Heart Ridge. When the Marines captured Tapochau, the Japanese retreated farther north. There Saito's men found themselves surrounded, and the general called on them to sacrifice themselves. "We must utilize this opportunity to exalt true Japanese manhood," he told his men, and promised to "deliver still another blow to the American devils and leave my bones on Saipan as a bulwark of the Pacific."

Saito had been wounded, and on July 6 committed seppuku, ritual suicide. The following morning, his men fulfilled his dying wish. Clutching guns, rusty bayonets, and clubs, they

THE PHOTOGRAPHER
W. Eugene Smith's image of Angelo Klonis during the battle for Saipan. Klonis, a Greek immigrant from Santa Fe, New Mexico, joined the military to gain U.S. citizenship. A different photo of the sergeant graced a 2002 U.S. postage stamp honoring Smith's work. Opposite: An islander father and his wounded child following the battle.

set out on a death charge. "It sounded like a big herd of cattle," one American recalled. "There were so many of them that the ground rumbled." Yelling "Banzai!" ("May you live 10,000 years!") their forces arrived en masse, with the two sides fighting hand to hand, until the Americans finally drove off the enemy with machine gun and howitzer fire. Three days later, U.S. forces secured the island, ending a battle that took the lives of 3,000 Americans and nearly 30,000 Japanese.

Saipan was the first invaded territory with more than a handful of civilians. Japanese troops had forbidden the islanders from surrendering, and with the defeat, many residents fled to Saipan's northern end. "American people are going to kill you, someday, somehow. It's better off dying than caught by American soldier," Koyu Shiroma's father warned him. Arriving at the Morubi Cliffs, the then five-year-old watched as neighbors leaped to their deaths. "So everybody jumping, so I just jump myself," recalled Shiroma.

"AMERICAN PEOPLE ARE GOING TO KILL YOU, SOMEDAY, SOMEHOW. IT'S BETTER OFF DYING THAN CAUGHT BY AMERICAN SOLDIER."

But when he plunged, he struck a tree. "I find I was hanging in a tree. Branch caught me . . . save me." As the islanders fell, the Americans frantically called out "trying to convince them that no harm would come to them," said Lieutenant William VanDusen. But all to no avail. As Shiroma dangled up high, he saw "other people jumping. Whole families jumping. Some people say, '*Hamnohaim banzai*' ['Long live the emperor']." Soldiers who had survived the battle then followed them over the edge or else blew themselves up with grenades. Below, bodies cluttered the surf. Instead of horrifying their fellow countrymen, all the suicides drew positive press in Japan, where Tokyo's *Yomiuri* newspaper praised "the pride of Japanese women," who killed themselves with their children.

Soon after Saipan fell so did Tinian and Guam. With those islands secured, Navy Seabees came in and transformed the islands into the largest air bases in the world. As the next part of Operation Forager, the Americans then set out to take the Palaus, some 600 miles to the southwest. "Waiting is a major part of war, but I never experienced any more supremely agonizing suspense than the excruciating torture of those moments," Marine corporal Eugene Sledge, a mortarman who braced for the September 15 invasion of the Palau island of Peleliu, would write in a 1981 memoir. "I broke out in a cold sweat as the tension mounted with the intensity of bombardment. My stomach was tied in knots. I had a lump in my throat and swallowed only with great difficulty. My knees nearly buckled, so I clung weakly to the side of the tractor. I felt

CONTINUED ON PAGE 58

CITIZENS DID THEIR BEST TO support the war effort. They had to conserve, and, like the woman at top, used ration coupons to buy meat and other necessities. To finance the war, the government ran War Loan Drives, as with the one to the right in New York's Times Square. For this 1944 drive, General Dwight D. Eisenhower implored citizens to give "so as to ensure that this conflict will be brought to the speediest possible conclusion and with the least loss in life." Above: USO workers filled boxes of supplies to ship to the troops overseas.

ZION NATIONAL
Coca-Cola
ARNOLD SOYA-NUT BREAD
HOTEL
BUY WAR BONDS
THREE FEATH
5TH WAR LOAN
$18,300,000
BALLROOM
CHOP SUEY
RIALTO
NEW HORROR HIT
"INVISIBLE MAN'S REVENG
JON HALL ALAN CURTIS
JOHN CARRADINE
REPUBLIC
AUTOMAT
FINEST FOOD
LOWEST POSSIBLE PRICES
CAFETERIA
HECTORS
FADA
5 EA

CONTINUED FROM PAGE 55

nauseated and feared that my bladder would surely empty and reveal me to be the coward I was."

Sledge's fears were well founded. On Peleliu, the Japanese had constructed tunnels throughout the island's volcanic network of rocky caves so their forces could be positioned above the surf and easily target enemy troops below. As the Marine headed out, he saw his friends mowed down. "I felt sickened to the depths of my soul," Sledge would recall. "I asked God, 'Why, why, why?' I turned my face away and wished that I were imagining it all. I had tasted the bitterest essence of the war, the sight of helpless comrades being slaughtered, and it filled me with disgust... We were expendable! It was difficult to accept. We come from a nation and a culture that values life and the individual. To find oneself in a situation where your life seems of little value is the ultimate in loneliness." The battle for Peleliu finally ended in November with Admiral Chester Nimitz's men capturing both that island and Angaur, just to its south. As many as 1,800 Americans died on Peleliu, a conquest that resulted in the military's highest-ever casualty rate for an amphibious assault.

And just as Marines like Sledge dealt with the daily terror of war, the folks at home waited and wondered, not knowing if their husbands, fathers, sons, fiancés, and friends were hunkered in a cold, wet trench with just a photo of a loved one for comfort, or lying dead on a deserted beach. Many people Stateside religiously read the papers, went to the cinema to watch the latest *March of Time,* Pathé, and Universal newsreels, and scanned maps in search of islands they had never heard of—some too small to be listed. And they mourned with neighbors who set gold stars in their windows for lost family members, all the while praying they would not earn a star of their own.

By then, Japan's defenses had been stretched thin, and the Allies struck everywhere they could. Flying was especially hazardous, and airmen accounted for almost a quarter of U.S. deaths. On September 2, 1944, Lieutenant George H.W. Bush piloted one of numerous planes that took off from the carrier *San Jacinto* for an attack on the island of Chichi-jima. With him flew Radioman John Delaney and Lieutenant Junior Grade William White. As they arrived at Chichi-jima, antiaircraft bullets struck their Avenger torpedo bomber. "Suddenly there was a jolt as if a massive fist had crunched into the belly of the plane," recalled Bush. "Smoke poured into the cockpit, and I could see flames rippling across the crease of the wing, edging toward the fuel tanks."

Despite the hit, Bush released four 500-pound bombs on the radio facility. There was no time to attempt a return to base in the hobbled craft, so the crew bailed out. As Bush jumped from the plane, he hit his head on the craft's tail. With his parachute damaged, he slammed into the water. Both Delaney and White died in the crash. Bleeding from his forehead, stung by poisonous jellyfish, and nauseated from swallowing saltwater, Bush pulled himself into his life raft and drifted for hours in the open sea. He was spotted seven miles from the island and rescued by the USS *Finback.* Many airmen on other planes who accompanied Bush's mission and survived their crashes were not as lucky. The Japanese tortured and killed them.

It wasn't just the enemy that Americans had to fear. Typhoon

CONTINUED ON PAGE 62

LIEUTENANT GEORGE H.W. BUSH was rescued by sailors aboard the submarine *Finback* after Japanese artillery shot down his bomber near Chichi-jima. Bush was the only member of his crew to survive the 1944 mission.

Soon after the destruction of Manila, Carl Mydans made his way through the city with his camera.

WAR SEEN THROUGH HIS LENS

LIFE photographer Carl Mydans endured imprisonment at the hands of the Japanese, and following his release he captured some of the war's most iconic images

THE LIFE MAGAZINE WRITER-photographer team of Carl and Shelley Mydans headed to China in 1941 to cover the Second Sino-Japanese War. Their piece "Defenders of the Philippines" had just arrived in New York when the Japanese bombed Pearl Harbor. Like thousands of other foreign nationals, the couple was tossed into Manila's Santo Tomás University internment camp and were soon shipped to a camp in Shanghai. Then, in 1943, the Mydanses became part of a rare prisoner exchange, returning home aboard the Swedish repatriation ship *Gripsholm* with the likes of the British adventurer turned Chinese general Morris "Two-Gun" Cohen and the *New Yorker* writer Emily Hahn.

After photographing a Japanese American internment camp in California, Mydans set out to cover the Allied liberation of France and Italy. He then returned to the Pacific. Mydans was the only still photographer present as General Douglas MacArthur waded onto the beach on Luzon in January 1945. He recalled how when MacArthur's landing craft neared the shore it suddenly went into reverse. The general didn't want to be seen landing on a steel pontoon, insisting on triumphantly walking through the surf. "No one I have ever known in public life had a better understanding of the drama and power of a picture," said Mydans of MacArthur and what is one of the best-known photographs from the war. (See pages 62–63.)

Mydans covered the battle for Manila, and took part in the February 1945 freeing of friends from Santo Tomás, an assignment he called "the most important story of my life." He then found an ideal vantage point atop a 40mm gun turret on the USS *Missouri* to photograph MacArthur as he accepted the Japanese surrender. Mydans watched as Foreign Minister Mamoru Shigemitsu limped forward on his wooden leg. "He leaned on his cane, took off his top hat, and stripped off his gloves, and for an instant seemed confused," Mydans, who died at 97 in 2004, recalled. "As I watched this man, at what for him must have been a terrible moment, I suddenly felt all my pent-up wartime anger drain away, and compassion filled my heart."

LUCKY
LEGS II

AMERICAN TROOPS USED A Sherman tank for cover, left, as they advanced on Japanese positions on Bougainville in March 1944. Above: Corporal Henry Blake Jr., left, and Private First Class George Kirk, two Navajo members of the U.S. Marines during the battle for that island. The men belonged to an elite group called Code Talkers who served in the Pacific, European, and African theaters. Using such Native American languages as Navajo, Hopi, and Comanche, they sent messages that the enemy was unable to decipher.

CONTINUED FROM PAGE 58

Cobra hit Admiral William Halsey's Third Fleet in December 1944. Massive waves broke against the ships. When Captain Stuart H. Ingersoll sounded general quarters on his carrier, the USS *Monterey,* Lieutenant Gerald Ford headed to the pilothouse. Just then a 70-foot-high wave hit the ship and pitched the vessel 25 degrees to port, nearly knocking the 31-year-old overboard. As the storm battered the *Monterey,* Ford recalled, planes on the hangar deck hit one another and the bulkheads "like pinballs." The pounding set off the gas tanks, and the flames shot below deck. Ingersoll had been ordered to abandon ship, but he said, "We can fix this." Ford put on a gas mask and headed below with a fire brigade. While aircraft blew up on deck, the lieutenant and his men put out fires, rescued the injured, and saved their ship from a storm that capsized three destroyers, damaged a dozen others, and took the lives of 793 men.

"I HAD TASTED THE BITTEREST ESSENCE OF THE WAR...AND IT FILLED ME WITH DISGUST." —CORPORAL EUGENE SLEDGE

As Nimitz took the Palau islands, MacArthur, as part of Operation Tradewind, captured Morotai in the Dutch East Indies' Molucca Islands, south of the Philippines. MacArthur then prepared to head north for the Philippine island of Leyte. On October 20, Admiral Halsey, whose motto was "Hit hard, hit fast, hit often," started setting men down on Leyte's east coast. In the midst of this, MacArthur triumphantly waded ashore with his officers and men, broadcasting on the radio that he had made good on his famous vow: "People of the Philippines, I have returned!"

The Allies, however, were not aware that the Japanese had set in place their plan Sho-Go, or Operation Victory. Admiral Soemu Toyoda oversaw the combined fleet and sent a decoy fleet to the north. He wanted to draw the Americans away from the San Bernardino Strait between Luzon and Samar Islands and then sought to attack the U.S. forces landing on Leyte. But American submarines of the U.S. Seventh Fleet realized it was a ruse, and on October 23 sank two heavy cruisers. Two days later three major engagements were fought, with battleships and cruisers, forcing the Japanese to withdraw.

Aware that conventional tactics could not stop the Americans, the Japanese decided to dispatch a group of pilots who would crash their planes into their enemy's ships. They were called kamikaze, "divine wind," a reference to a typhoon that saved Japan from a Mongol invasion in 1281. Captain Motoharu Okamura devised the suicidal approach, stating, "I firmly believe that the only way to swing the war in our favor is to resort to crash-dive attacks with our planes."

A group of 24 pilots prepared on October 25 to target the American ships. Knowing that their noble demise would earn them an honored spot at Yasukuni, the great Shinto shrine in Tokyo, the aviators first shared a toast and then climbed into their planes and flew to their deaths. Despite the assaults, by the end of December the Americans had secured both Leyte and the island of Mindoro to the south.

Those kamikazes would not be the last. Many who followed would sing the nationalistic song "Umi Yukaba" before they took to the air.

FULFILLING HIS PROMISE, General Douglas MacArthur, right, returned to the Philippines. Bottom left: An instructor explained to Japanese pilots how to carry out a kamikaze attack. Bottom right: Lieutenant Shigeo Naka received sake supplied by Emperor Hirohito before his suicide mission on Leyte.

614

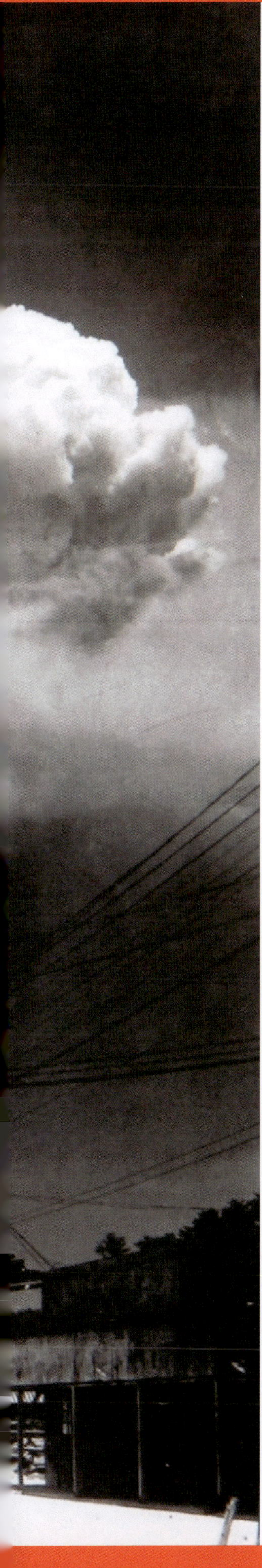

4

THE AMERICAN ROAD TO VICTORY

1945

WITH MUCH OF JAPAN SMOLDERING, THE UNITED STATES PREPARED FOR AN INVASION OF JAPAN, AND FINALLY ENDED THE WAR BY UNLEASHING THE NEW AND DEVASTATING ATOMIC BOMB

THE MUSHROOM CLOUD from the atomic bomb as it engulfed Nagasaki on the morning of August 9, 1945.

B

BY THE START OF 1945, THE U.S. MILITARY had largely destroyed Japan's ability to wage war. American forces had sent much of the empire's navy and merchant fleet to the bottom of the Pacific; naval advances had cut off their access to oil, steel, and food; and more than one million Japanese troops had been killed.

On January 9, General Douglas MacArthur's forces had moved from the Philippine islands of Leyte and Mindanao and landed on the island of Luzon. Rear Admiral Sanji Iwabuchi braced for their arrival in Manila, where he prepared a scorched-earth welcome, planting mines, constructing barricades of cars and trucks, and building pillboxes. As the fighting began, his troops bayonetted babies, and raped and slaughtered thousands of women. To capture the city, the American and Filipino forces had to fight house to house and use artillery. "It was like a bowling alley over our heads, guns shooting first from one side then from another," wrote the author John Dos Passos, who served as a war correspondent. When Manila was finally secured in March, the city known as the Pearl of the Orient lay in ruins and more than 100,000 civilians had been killed. Those released from Japanese prison and internment camps

A PLATOON OF AMERICAN soldiers advanced through the blasted ruins of the Intramuros—Manila's ancient walled city—which saw some of the heaviest fighting between U.S. and Japanese forces.

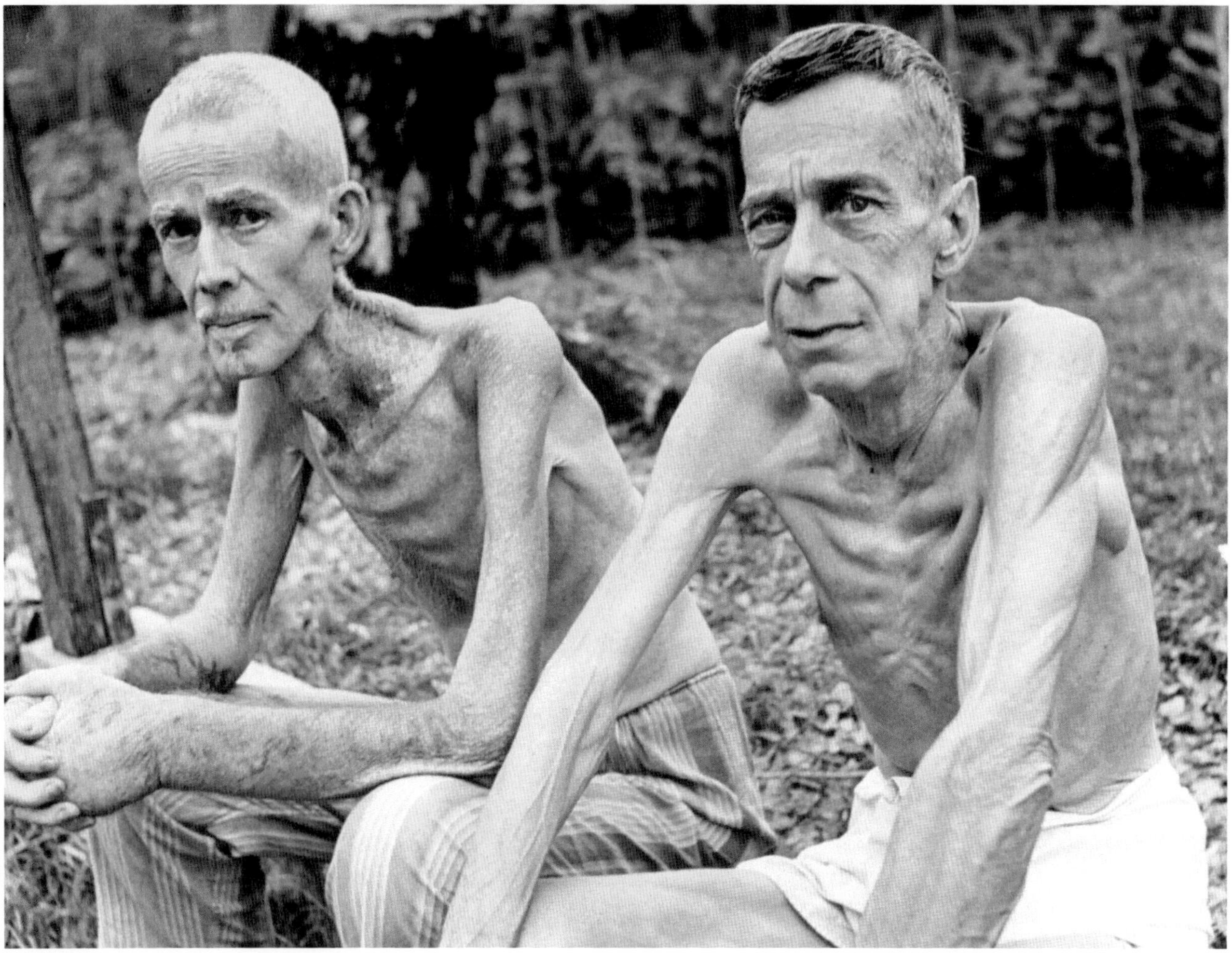

like Santo Tomás, where the nurses and others from Bataan were held, looked skeletal. "I got out, and there [were] all these American soldiers," Georgia native Mildred Manning recalled. "I thought I'd go nuts. Everybody was about to go nuts. I found me a soldier from Georgia and hugged him. That's the first thing I did!"

Surrender was not a choice for the Japanese—indeed, the word didn't even exist in their dictionary. With his options dwindling and believing the Americans were planning an invasion of Tokyo, Emperor Hirohito approved operation Ketsu-Go, calling on his people to nobly fight to the death, and if necessary to become kamikazes. Though Admiral William Halsey called those suicide fliers "the only weapon I feared in the war," they could not stop the Americans. The Army Air Corps had already started bombing Japan in June 1944. And with the capture of the Mariana Islands, Tinian had become the jumping off point for B-29 Superfortress missions. In January 1945, General Curtis LeMay, who had become the main proponent of strategic bombing in Germany, took over there.

But Tinian was more than just a base for "Old Iron Pants" LeMay's bomber pilots. The island also became the headquarters for the 509th Composite Group, which was tasked with dropping the Manhattan Project's atomic weapon. Lieutenant Colonel Paul W. Tibbets Jr. commanded the unit, and to maintain secrecy, none of his men knew their ultimate mission. As Second Lieutenant Jack Widowsky remembered, they were warned, "You don't discuss with anyone where you are, who you are, what you're doing... [not with] your wife, your mother, your sister, your girlfriend, or anything."

As the next step in their advance on Japan, the Americans set their sights on Iwo Jima. The tear-shaped island lay halfway between Tinian and Japan and would give pilots easier access to the enemy homeland. Iwo Jima was an inhospitable spit of earth covered with ash and hundreds of caves. The emperor had personally instructed Lieutenant General Tadamichi Kuribayashi to make a final stand, and Kuribayashi told his commanders that every man must "resist until the end, making his position his tomb." His 21,000 troops thus honeycombed the island with tunnels, while setting up blockhouses, pillboxes, and hidden artillery pieces.

The U.S. Navy started shelling on February 19, and American

AMERICAN AND FILIPINO civilians cheered their liberation from the Japanese prison camp at Santo Tomás University, opposite. Conditions there were brutal, as seen with these emaciated American civilians above, Lee Rogers, left, and John C. Todd.

forces landed under the command of Major General Harry Schmidt. They planned to quickly take the island. But their bombing did little to dislodge the Japanese entrenched in Mount Suribachi, who greeted the Marines with a pummeling of bullets and mortars. Kuribayashi also sent out kamikaze pilots. Even so, the Marines would not be deterred; on the 23rd they took Suribachi, and raised the Stars and Stripes. Lieutenant Colonel Chandler Johnson, though, felt the flag planted at the summit was not large enough to both inspire his men and demoralize the enemy, so he had them hoist a second larger flag. That raising was caught by Associated Press photographer Joe Rosenthal. As the banner unfurled, *Time*'s Robert Sherrod reported, "a lot of the boys cried." Soon Rosenthal's photo appeared in newspapers across America and became a symbol of unity in the dread struggle. It remains arguably the most iconic wartime image in U.S. history.

TROOPS COULD NOT DISLODGE the enemy from their Iwo Jima compounds and had to blow up caves, left. Above: This naval lieutenant surrendered after hearing a broadcast by one of his comrades telling of his good treatment at the hands of the Americans.

Even with the mountain conquered, Schmidt's forces still faced an implacable foe. As the Japanese shot at them from their hideouts, the Marines responded with flame throwers and grenades. When that failed, they pumped in gasoline and sea water. Most Japanese still refused to surrender. As pilot Omagari Satoru mused, "Even the dead were being forced to fight." Yet they could not withstand the U.S. onslaught, and the Americans conquered the island on March 26.

Before he died and Iwo Jima fell, Kuribayashi learned that the Americans had firebombed Tokyo, where his family lived. Up until then, LeMay's forces had conducted high-altitude raids on the Japanese capital. The pressurized B-29s were well suited for such missions. They were the most advanced bomber of the time, equipped with a 20mm cannon, 12 .50-caliber machine guns, and several remote-controlled gun turrets, and could carry at least a dozen men and 10 tons of bombs. But initial attacks had limited success targeting sites, so the cigar-chomping

CONTINUED ON PAGE 74

TROOPS ADVANCED DURING the battle for Iwo Jima, top. Above: During the attempt to take the island, Marines crawled up a slope on Red Beach No. 1 toward Mount Suribachi. After the Americans conquered the mount, the troops raised a flag, right. "The sky was overcast," recalled AP photographer Joe Rosenthal, who took an iconic shot of the event. "The wind just whipped the flag out over the heads of the group, and at their feet the disrupted terrain and the broken stalks of the shrubbery exemplified the turbulence of war."

CONTINUED FROM PAGE 71

general controversially suggested low-level bombing. They were also to carry jellied-gasoline firebombs made from the newly devised napalm to incinerate their targets.

The first such mission took off on March 9, with 325 B-29s heading out to destroy airplane-parts factories in the Tokyo suburb of Shitamachi. Pilot Robert Rodenhouse recalled how many of the city's wood and tar paper buildings simply ignited: "When we got over the target, it was like a thousand Christmas trees lit up all over." Yoshiko Hashimoto also vividly remembered that night. "Warehouses lined up on both sides of the river were burning. Women's hair and men's clothes caught on fire. My mother took off her protective hood from her head, put it on my head, and looked into my eyes. Without a protective hood, my mother's hair must have caught on fire after I jumped into the river. She must have died in agony."

"THE SMELL OF PEARL HARBOR FIRES IS TOO PERSISTENT IN OUR NOSTRILS." —GENERAL CURTIS LEMAY

The attack killed 100,000 people and destroyed 267,000 buildings, making it the most destructive bombing raid of the war. LeMay showed little sympathy: "We don't pause to shed any tears for uncounted hordes of Japanese who lie charred in that acrid-smelling rubble. The smell of Pearl Harbor fires is too persistent in our nostrils." With the triumph of that bombing run, the general planned raids on such cities as Osaka, Kobe, and Nagoya, and Foreign Minister Mamoru Shigemitsu could only lament, "Day by day, Japan turned into a furnace."

With Iwo Jima captured, the Americans prepared for the even more daunting Operation Iceberg. They sought Okinawa, the largest of the Ryukyu Islands, as a base to launch a ground invasion of Japan 350 miles away. To lure the Americans into a trap, Lieutenant General Mitsura Ushijima fortified the island with steel garrisons and set his 100,000 troops in caves and tunnels throughout the mountainous ridges. And he conscripted the nearly half million residents to fight alongside them with bamboo spears. Calling for total obedience, the troops even had inhabitants on the nearby Kerama, Zamami, and Tokashiki islands commit mass suicide.

For the battle, the Americans dispatched the largest fleet ever, made up of more than 40 carriers, 18 battleships, 200 destroyers, and 200,000 troops, and softened up the island's defenses with air and sea attacks. Lieutenant General Simon Bolivar Buckner Jr.—who liked to offer the toast "May you walk in the ashes of Tokyo"—landed on April 1. By nightfall he had brought 50,000 men ashore. Surprisingly, for five days the Americans encountered no shooting. Then on April 6, the Battle of Okinawa began, a clash that became known as the Typhoon of Steel. Three hundred fifty planes streaked toward the American fleet, the first of 10 such waves. The Japanese also launched piloted cruise missiles released by planes. They likewise dispatched Kairyu subs that rammed ships, and suicide frogmen with explosives attached to their suits.

One such attack proved especially devastating. Just after 10 on the morning of May 11, Japanese Sub-lieutenant Yasunori Seizo flew his Zero through the clouds and released a 550-pound bomb above the USS *Bunker Hill*'s

CONTINUED ON PAGE 79

WITH AIR BASES NEARBY, American bombers easily reached cities in Japan, as with these 52 planes passing near Mount Fuji on their way to Tokyo. The firebombing of that city, bottom left and right, proved devastating.

220
1415
1265

AMERICAN SHIPS TOOK A beachhead on Okinawa, left, a battle that Corporal William Manchester recalled had left the island "a cratered moonscape," causing troops to live in "one vast cesspool. Mingled with that stench was another—the corrupt and corrupting odor of rotting human flesh." Eleven Okinawans, including this mother and child, top, emerged from a cave after being assured that no harm would come to them. American troops, above, listened to a radio report on the unconditional surrender of Germany.

CONTINUED FROM PAGE 74

flight deck. It exploded as his plane slammed into 34 armed and fueled aircraft, setting off a chain reaction of explosions. Thirty seconds later a plane flown by Ensign Ogawa Kiyoshi dropped another bomb and likewise crashed into the carrier. As a third plane neared, gunners took it down with machine gun fire. More than 370 men perished from those kamikaze attacks, and as fire crews tried to contain the blazes, other planes attempted to destroy the ship.

Meanwhile, troops fighting it out on Okinawa were buffeted by fierce, drenching monsoons. Naval and air bombardment as well as smoke grenades could not dislodge the Japanese, so the Americans simply dynamited caves. The men were tasked with capturing spots they nicknamed Chocolate Drop Hill and Flattop, and advanced with flame-throwing tanks. "All night, every night, shells erupted close enough to shake the mud beneath you at the rate of five or six a minute," wrote Corporal William Manchester. His unit tried to wrest Sugar Loaf Hill from the enemy: "If you were fortunate enough to reach the top, you encountered the Japanese defenders, almost face to face . . . Japanese bayonets were fixed; ours weren't. We used the knives, or, in my case, a .45 revolver and M1 carbine. The mud beneath our feet was deeply veined with blood. It was slippery. Blood is very slippery. So you skidded around, in deep shock, fighting as best you could until one side outnumbered the other."

Throughout, Manchester recalled, "You could hear the cries of the dying but could do nothing." Medics struggled to aid the wounded. Desmond Doss's battalion was fighting on a cliff they called Hacksaw Ridge. At the top massed thousands of Japanese who assaulted them with a seemingly unrelenting barrage of firepower. At one point only Doss and the wounded remained. Despite also being injured, the unarmed medic treated his comrades and over a number of hours lowered them one by one down the cliff to safety, rescuing 75 soldiers.

When the men entered communities, some families used hand grenades to kill themselves. Ruth Miyara and 45 other student nurses took refuge in a cave with Japanese soldiers. "We were told not to be captured," recalled Miyara. When the Americans warned them that the cave would be blown up, the Japanese troops fired at them. The Americans then tossed in a grenade. "I clung to the rugged rocks and raised my head only to be choked. Everybody started streaming, 'Mother help me. Father help me. Teacher help me, I can't breathe. Help, help.'" Miyara doesn't recall waking up, but a friend told her she was found under a pile of dead bodies, one of only seven student nurses to survive.

Major fighting on Okinawa was over by the end of June, leaving about 100,000 Japanese and more than 12,000 Americans dead, including General

FOLLOWING THE DEATH OF Franklin D. Roosevelt, Navy Chief Petty Officer Graham Jackson played "Goin' Home," opposite, bottom left. FDR's coffin was transported through Washington, D.C., opposite, top, while mourners wept, below. Above, Winston Churchill, left, Harry Truman, and Josef Stalin in Potsdam, Germany.

Buckner, the highest-ranking U.S. officer killed in the war. Like many of his comrades, Marine corporal Eugene Sledge had been buffeted by the stress of battle. He had fought on Okinawa for the entire 82-day campaign, and found the fight "characterized by confusion, awesome violence, gripping fear, physical stress and fatigue, fierce hatred of the enemy, and overwhelming grief over the loss of friends." He saw the barbarity that humans could be driven to, and became stunned by how he and others had become "reduced to a brutish existence in their fight for survival amid the violent death, terror, tension, fatigue, and filth that was the infantryman's war."

In the midst of the battle, President Franklin Roosevelt died on April 12 in Warm Springs, Georgia. Adolf Hitler committed suicide two weeks later in Berlin. Germany then surrendered on May 7. Victory in Europe meant the end of Hitler's imagined Thousand-Year Reich, which actually survived a mere 12 years, though it caused the death of tens of millions. Vice President Harry Truman found himself thrust into the presidency, and the Joint Chiefs briefed him on the plan to invade Japan. The operation would need several million soldiers, and the generals and admirals had no illusions about what they would face. Japanese officers like Pearl Harbor commander Mitsuo Fuchida—whom Tokyo dispatched to Hiroshima—were charged with organizing the stand, with officials telling troops, "Every soldier should fight to the last moment believing in the final victory." They armed men, women, and children with weapons, shovels, and sharpened bamboo poles. One girl recalled being told, "If you don't kill at least one enemy soldier, you don't deserve to die."

In July, Truman, Prime Minister Winston Churchill, and Soviet premier Josef Stalin met in Potsdam, Germany, and issued a declaration calling for Japan's immediate and unconditional surrender. Japanese leaders ignored the ultimatum. Knowing an invasion might lead to the deaths of a million American servicemen, Truman, just months into his presidency, faced the daunting decision about using the newly completed atomic bomb. Fully aware of encounters with the Japanese at places like Tarawa, where only 17 of the 4,836 there did not fight to the death, or Saipan, where civilians plunged from cliffs yelling, "Long live the emperor," he knew he had to end the war as quickly as possible.

After years of work, the Manhattan Project finally tested an atomic weapon on the morning of July 16. A crew set a bomb nicknamed the Gadget in the Alamogordo Bombing and Gunnery Range south of Los Alamos, New Mexico. Program head J. Robert Oppenheimer named the spot Trinity. It alluded to a poem by the 17th-century British poet John Donne that was beloved by Oppenheimer's former girlfriend Jean Tatlock—who had committed suicide the year before—and included these lines:

Batter my heart, three-personed
God; for you
As yet but knock, breathe, shine,
and seek to mend;
That I may rise and stand,
o'erthrow me, and bend
Your force to break, blow, burn,
and make me new.

Detonated at 5:29 a.m., Gadget produced an intense burst of light as its flames turned the New Mexico sand into glass and shot a mushroom cloud 40,000 feet into the sky. "We knew the world would not be the same," recalled Oppenheimer of those moments. "A few people laughed. A few people cried. Most people were silent. I remembered

CONTINUED ON PAGE 84

J. ROBERT OPPENHEIMER and Lieutenant General Leslie Groves, leaders of the Manhattan Project, examined the aftereffects of the atomic bomb test at Alamogordo, New Mexico.

A checkpoint leading to Project Y, the secret Los Alamos site where the atomic bomb was created.

THE BIRTHPLACE OF THE BOMB

The top-secret development of the atomic weapon in the mesas of New Mexico was hidden in plain sight

WHILE 5,000 PEOPLE LIVED and worked there, Los Alamos did not officially exist. The New Mexican "secret city" is 96 miles north of Albuquerque and 16 miles from the nearest town and was established by the Manhattan Project to carry out Project Y, the effort to harness the power of nuclear fission and create an atomic bomb. Built on a group of mesas and called "the Hill" by locals, Los Alamos was sheltered behind gates and guard towers and defended by Army soldiers.

Manhattan Project director Lieutenant General Leslie Groves tasked theoretical physicist J. Robert Oppenheimer with running the Hill. Oppenheimer, who is known as the "father of the atomic bomb," set it up like a college campus in order to foster an academic community and the free exchange of ideas. Not only did Los Alamos have its own research labs, schools, churches, hospital, and theaters, but there were also particle accelerators, Van de Graaff generators, and a cyclotron. All was arranged so that physicists, metallurgists, explosives experts, chemists, and engineers recruited from universities and industries in the United States and Great Britain could work in peace as they raced against the Nazis' Uranverein—Uranium Club—and the Japanese Ni-Go project. But unlike their Axis bomb-building counterparts, Project Y workers could head out with their spouses and children for a swim, a hike, and even ski runs.

The Hill had just one address—Post Office Box 1663—which appeared on all driver's licenses as well as birth certificates. Not surprisingly, such a large refuge filled with families drew its share of attention. Many locals wondered what really went on behind the fences; deliverymen from Sears & Roebuck couldn't understand why they had dropped off a dozen baby bassinets at just one post office box. Fearing lips might be loosened—say, when residents went for drinks to La Fonda, a popular Santa Fe watering hole—agents monitored residents. And to play it safe, Oppenheimer had staffers spread the rumor that the folks who lived at the Hill were developing electric rockets—not the most devastating weapon in human history.

COLONEL PAUL W. TIBBETS JR. aboard the B-29 bomber *Enola Gay*—which he named for his mother—before taking off for Hiroshima. Opposite, top: The mushroom cloud created by the bomb called Little Boy as it rose above Hiroshima. Following the bombing, the Jesuit priest John Siemes said that "a procession of people begins to stream up the valley from the city . . . Their steps are dragging, their faces blackened. Many are bleeding or have suffered burns." Bottom: The city a few months after the bombing.

CONTINUED FROM PAGE 80

the line from the Hindu scripture the Bhagavad Gita . . . 'Now I am become death, the destroyer of worlds.' I suppose we all felt that, one way or another."

With two bombs prepared, the question was what city to attack. Hiroshima was the first chosen. The components for a bomb called Little Boy and fueled by uranium-235 were rushed to Tinian. They set the weapon on Paul Tibbets's *Enola Gay* and headed out on the morning of August 6.

Unlike other cities, Hiroshima had been spared bombings. Planes regularly flew overhead and citizens ran to shelters but soon came out to a city unscathed. It was the same on that morning. Following the all-clear siren, crowds headed back to their breakfasts and rushed to their jobs. Hatsuyo Nakamura, the widow of a tailor killed in Singapore at the start of the war, was cooking some rice and reading a copy of the Hiroshima newspaper *Chugoku*. She then gave some peanuts to her children, son Toshio, 10, and daughters Yaeko, eight, and Myeko, five.

"SHOULD WE CONTINUE TO FIGHT . . . IT WOULD LEAD TO THE TOTAL EXTINCTION OF HUMAN CIVILIZATION." —EMPEROR HIROHITO

Few saw the *Enola Gay,* nearly six miles above the city, though some recalled noticing a plummeting black object. The bomb, aimed at a Japanese army headquarters, burst 1,890 feet above the surface, releasing an inferno that spread out over 4.4 square miles. As copilot Captain Robert Lewis watched its explosion, he wrote in his logbook, "My God, what have we done?"

One Hiroshiman recalled how "the sky split open over the city." At the explosion's center, the temperature approached 5,432 degrees Fahrenheit. As many as 80,000 people died instantly. Bodies simply vaporized, often leaving ghostly white shadows across the ground. Nakamura's home lay three-quarters of a mile from the epicenter. She recalled a flash of white light, and found herself flung across the room. She then heard Myeko cry out, "Mother, help me!" Timbers and tiles buried her youngest child, and Nakamura frantically dug her out. She then heard crying, "*Tasukete! Tasukete!* (Help! Help!)" and pulled out her other children. As they emerged from their shattered home, Nakamura could not answer Myeko's questions: "Why is it night already?" "Why did our house fall down?" "What happened?" Naval Surgeon Taira Ake arrived in Hiroshima that afternoon and found hundreds dying on the northern edge. "They didn't look like human beings," said the lieutenant. "The flesh was burned from their faces and hands, and many were blinded and deaf."

Three days later the bomber *Bockscar,* piloted by Major Charles Sweeny, took off with a bomb dubbed Fat Man (reportedly because of its resemblance to the *Maltese Falcon* character played by rotund actor Sydney Greenstreet). Fat Man, fueled by plutonium-239, was more powerful than Little Boy. The crew headed toward Kokura. But cloud covering made it difficult to see that city, so they flew southwest to Nagasaki. "We saw this big plume climbing up, up into the sky," recalled bombardier Charles Levy. "It was purple, red, white, all the colors—something like boiling coffee, it looked alive." Perhaps, but it brought only death, to an estimated 40,000 to 75,000 souls.

By then the Allied bombing raids had partially or totally destroyed 64 cities and killed more than one million people. Fearing complete destruction and an invasion by the Soviets, who had declared war on Japan on August 8, 1945, and invaded Manchuria, Hirohito announced Japan's surrender. His August 14 radio broadcast was the first time most Japanese had heard the voice of their god-king, many bowing as he spoke. The emperor told his nation,

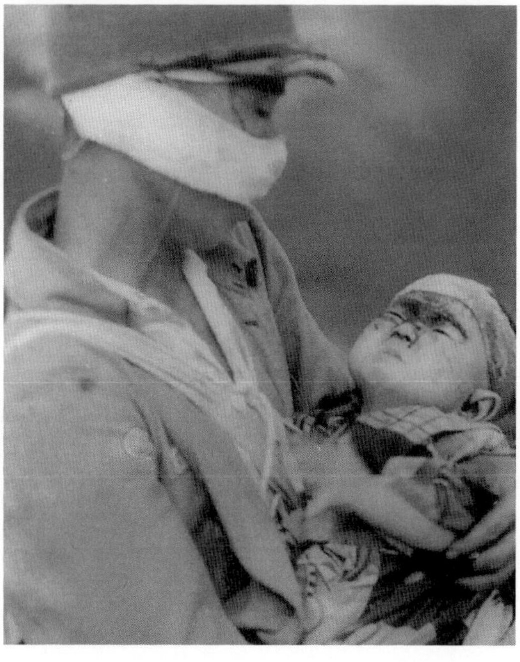

AN ATOMIC BOMB DEVASTATED Nagasaki three days after Hiroshima. It destroyed areas like this one, above, four miles from the explosion's epicenter. Many of those not killed by the atomic bombs endured horrible burns or high rates of cancer and other life-threatening ailments.

"Should we continue to fight it would not only result in the ultimate collapse and obliteration of the Japanese nation but also it would lead to the total extinction of human civilization."

While Oppenheimer at Alamogordo had viewed his weapon as the embodiment of the vengeful Hindu god Shiva, for the Americans the devastation of Hiroshima and Nagasaki was as if the two other members of the Hindu trinity, Brahma, the Creator, and Vishnu, the Preserver, had intervened for the Allies and created peace. "You couldn't believe how happy we were. It was like getting a death sentence revoked," said Marine George Niland who had just fought on Okinawa. "You know, it just—it was wonderful."

On September 2 aboard the USS *Missouri* in Tokyo Bay, delegates from the Allied powers watched as Foreign Minister Mamoru Shigemitsu and Army Chief of Staff General Yoshijiro Umezu signed the unconditional surrender document for the Japanese. British General Arthur Percival and American General Jonathan Wainwright, who had both just been released from prison camp, stood behind MacArthur as the general added his signature. MacArthur then handed the first of the pens used to Wainwright and the second to Percival. Afterward, Admiral Chester Nimitz signed, as did representatives of other nations.

The next day, soldiers escorted General Tomoyuki Yamashita—the Tiger of Malaya, who in early 1942 had captured Singapore from Percival and later the Philippines, where Wainwright had surrendered—to Baguio, north of Manila. As he entered the room to surrender he was stunned to see the American and British generals, both of whom had been imprisoned, and whose troops his men had mistreated and murdered. After he was read the Instrument of Surrender, there was a long hesitation until Yamashita was asked, "Are you ready to sign the surrender document?" He responded, "I am." Afterward he tried to shake Percival's hand. The general refused. ●

THE JAPANESE DELEGATION, led by Foreign Minister Mamoru Shigemitsu (front left, in top hat) and Army Chief of Staff General Yoshijiro Umezu, arrived on the USS *Missouri* in Tokyo Bay, to sign the Instrument of Surrender. From the battleship's foremast fluttered the flag that flew above the U.S. Capitol on December 7, 1941.

SERVICEMEN IN HAWAII— where it all started nearly four years earlier—thrilled to the news on August 15, 1945, that the Japanese had finally surrendered.

THE AFTERMATH

THE ROAD TO PEACE AND RECONCILIATION

In the years after World War II, Japan slowly recovered from its defeat and became an ally of the United States. Yet memories of nearly four years of battle still haunt many Americans who fought there and have since tried to make peace with their experiences

THE AMERICANS, THE BRITISH, THE FRENCH, the Chinese, the Koreans, and citizens of many other nations were ecstatic over the end of World War II. But no one could forget that victory came at a horrible cost, a globe-spanning conflict that lasted eight years and took the lives of some 70 million to 85 million people. And during this country's three and a half years at war, more than 416,000 Americans died, over 100,000 of them in the Pacific.

With the war finally over, those imprisoned by Japan gained their freedom. Of the 27,000 Americans held, 40 percent had perished in captivity, compared to 1 percent of POWs held by Nazi Germany. The Japanese routinely brutalized and killed prisoners, and they worked many relentlessly. Lester Tenney, who had been captured on Bataan, was forced to shovel coal for 12 hours a day. In return, his captors fed him only three bowls of rice a day. The nurses from Bataan subsisted on less, causing Mildred Manning to lose all her teeth from a lack of nutrition.

Following his release, General Jonathan Wainwright suffered from depression, blaming himself for the loss of the Philippines. On his arrival in Washington, D.C., however, he was disabused of that idea and whisked to the Capitol to speak to a joint session of Congress. From there, Wainwright headed to the White House, and in the Rose Garden President Harry Truman awarded him the Medal of Honor. That November, his hometown of Walla Walla, Washington—where during his captivity the community had named a street in his honor—feted him. He died September 2, 1953, eight years to the day after the surrender aboard the USS *Missouri.*

Most of the 16 million men and women who served just wanted to get back to their old lives. These members of what has been dubbed the Greatest Generation returned to a nation experiencing an economic boom. Between 1944 and 1956, some 10 million veterans took advantage of the GI Bill to attend trade schools and colleges. This allowed them to advance both financially and socially, thus spurring the development of a solid middle class. Many raised families, sought the American dream, and were drawn to new developments in places like Levittown, New York, where they could put down roots and mow lawns on little parcels of suburban heaven. The nation also saw the start of the movement for equality for women and African Americans.

Ronald Oba, who had watched the Japanese bomb Pearl Harbor and served with the Japanese American 442nd Regimental Combat Team, studied physical therapy and became a hospital administrator in Hawaii. He died in 2017, at the age of 94. Desmond Doss became the first conscientious objector to receive the Medal of Honor, and then settled down to a farm in Rising Fawn, Georgia, where he died at 87 in 2006. Manning married and continued nursing in Jacksonville, Florida. When she died in 2013, age 98, she was the last known female POW of World War II.

Daniel Inouye also served in the 442nd, the most decorated unit of its size and length of service in American history. He was one of its 21 members

SOLDIERS OF THE 37TH Infantry "Buckeye" Division, who fought on Luzon and elsewhere in the Pacific, arrived in San Francisco in December 1945, above. After the war, many veterans took advantage of the GI Bill. This serviceman and his family, left, lived at the University of Iowa in a trailer village that was set up for vets and their families.

to receive a Medal of Honor. Having lost his right arm during a battle in Italy, he could no longer become a surgeon as he had dreamed, so Inouye studied political science and in 1963 entered the United States Senate. He died in 2012, age 88. Lieutenant John F. Kennedy earned the Navy and Marine Corps Medal as well as a Purple Heart and parlayed his wartime heroics into a political career—one cut short at the summit by his assassination at 46 in 1963. The coconut with his carved rescue message served as a paperweight on JFK's Oval Office desk. Gerald Ford retired from the Navy as a lieutenant commander, entered Congress, was appointed Vice President, and assumed the presidency upon Richard Nixon's resignation in 1974. Ford died in 2006, age 93. George H.W. Bush, who received the Distinguished Flying Cross, also served in Congress and rose to the White House. Like Ford, Bush was one of the nation's longest-lived chief executives, dying at 94 in 2018.

Hoping to prevent the instability that came with the end of World War I and eventually sparked World War II, America set out to rebuild many of the world's shattered societies and economies. President Truman made General George C. Marshall secretary of state, in which role he helped revive western and southern Europe. The President likewise charged Douglas MacArthur with transforming Japan. The general dismantled its army, forced Emperor Hirohito to renounce his divine status, set in place a new constitution, established reforms, broke up conglomerates, and created a parliamentary system that gave rights to women.

Just as in Europe, where the Nuremberg Trials brought some of the Nazis to justice, MacArthur oversaw the Tokyo War Crimes Trials. Prime Minister Hideki Tojo who led his nation into war; Commander Iwane Matsui, who ordered the slaughters in Nanjing; and General Tomoyuki Yamashita, who captured the Philippines and Malaysia, were all found guilty and executed. So were Lieutenant General Masaharu Homma, who commanded Japanese forces in Bataan, along with Lieutenant General Yoshio Tachibana and others who murdered Allied troops captured after the Chichi-jima bombing run from which Bush escaped.

With the war's end, vast swaths of Japan lay in ruin. Homer Bigart of the *New York Herald-Tribune* visited Hiroshima the day after the surrender, and noted how in part of the city "there was only flat, appalling desolation." Slowly the country was rebuilt. In 1956, Japan joined the United Nations. Though the planned 1940 Tokyo Olympics never happened, the capital finally got to host the Games in 1964, an honor widely seen as a recognition of the nation's transformation. Yoshinori Sakai, a student who was born in Hiroshima on the August morning when the bomb ignited his city, lit the Olympic torch.

Immediately after the nuclear attacks, troubling questions arose about whether it was morally justified to unleash such a ghastly weapon—one, it has since been revealed, the Japanese had also tried to develop. Many, including Truman and General Paul Tibbets, who commanded the flight of the *Enola Gay,* never questioned its purpose. "I viewed my mission as one to save lives," Tibbets said almost 60 years later. "I didn't bomb Pearl Harbor. I didn't start the war, but I was going to finish it." Commander Mitsuo Fuchida, who did attack Pearl Harbor, resented what

WITH THE WAR OVER, soldiers in the American occupying force hoisted the Stars and Stripes at Atsugi Air Base, left. Following Japan's surrender, those who waged the war were prosecuted at war crimes trials, below.

Tibbets did. He had been stationed in Hiroshima, but was luckily summoned away right before the bomb dropped. His commanders then ordered him to inspect the devastation, and he was the only member of his party not to die from radiation poisoning. Following the surrender, he headed home to Kashihara, where he worked on his family's chicken farm.

Fuchida's hatred of America started to soften in 1947 when he was reunited with Kazuo Kanegasaki, his former flight engineer, who had been taken prisoner by the Americans. Kanegasaki spoke well of his treatment by his captors, beginning for Fuchida a process during which he came to recognize Japan's moral culpability for the war. Fuchida also converted to Christianity and became a missionary. Almost two decades after the conflict's end, on a visit to the United States he met Tibbets. The warrior turned missionary, who had sparked America's entry into World War II, told the general who ended it that he'd done the right thing by bombing Japan and averting incalculable slaughter. "Every man, woman, and child would have resisted that invasion," Fuchida said, "using sticks and stones if necessary."

Not surprisingly, both Hiroshima and Nagasaki set up peace parks, became centers of the anti–nuclear weapons movement, and each August hold solemn remembrances. Many in those cities have suffered from unusually high rates of leukemia and other cancers. In 1955, 12-year-old Sasaki Sadako came down with leukemia. While she was in a hospital in Hiroshima, her roommate told her that cranes are a symbol of longevity and happiness, and a folk belief holds that those who fold 1,000 origami cranes will be granted a wish. Sadako folded 1,300, yet her wish for a cure was not granted and she died that October. Sadako's efforts, though, inspired others, and Hiroshima dedicated a Children's Peace Monument in her honor. Every year millions of paper crane wishes are set at the monument.

Today, Japan is a peaceful and highly developed economic powerhouse. And while nine countries now possess nuclear weapons, the Japanese have held to their pacifistic path. But there are continuing struggles over the nation's acceptance of war guilt. Unlike Germany, which has made penance for its crimes and paid reparations, Japan has long been gripped by a collective denial. There is a sense in Japan that they were not the aggressors, and many politicians and scholars deny that their troops massacred civilians, brutalized women, or carried out biological experiments on prisoners.

The Greatest Generation, their baby boom children, and their grandchildren have found endless fascination in the Pacific war. In 1954, President Dwight D. Eisenhower, who led the troops in Europe, dedicated a Marine memorial in Arlington, Virginia, inspired by Joe Rosenthal's Iwo Jima flag-raising photograph. At the Smithsonian National Air and Space Museum in Chantilly, Virginia, stands the *Enola Gay,* while *Bockscar* resides at Dayton's National Museum of the United States Air Force. The interest in the war has been rewarded with such books as James Jones's *From Here to Eternity,* a 1951 novel based on the author's time in Pearl Harbor. Iris Chang's groundbreaking 1997 book, *The Rape of Nanking,* offers a harrowing account of the Japanese atrocities in that city. John Hersey's *Hiroshima,* published in 1946 in *The New Yorker,* recounts the lives of six of the city's survivors. Quite a few of those and other accounts have been made into films. Spencer Tracy starred in 1944's *Thirty Seconds over Tokyo* about the Doolittle Raid. The film adaptation of *From Here to Eternity* (1953) won eight Academy Awards. And Laura Hillebrand's bestselling 2010 book, *Unbroken,* about Louis Zamperini's tortured imprisonment by the Japanese, was turned into a film by Angelina Jolie in 2014.

In 2006 Clint Eastwood made *Flags of Our Fathers,* based on James Bradley's 2000 book about the men who hoisted the flag on Iwo Jima. Eastwood also took the unusual approach of creating a second movie, *Letters from Iwo Jima,* also released in 2006, which he filmed in English and Japanese. *Letters* presents a nuanced account of the battle as seen by the Japanese combatants, from a private who would survive the onslaught to General Tadamichi Kuribayashi, who would not.

Kuribayashi's grandson, Yoshitaka Shindo, was born 13 years following his grandfather's death. He met with Eastwood as he planned the film, and was pleased to learn of the director's desire to tell the story of the battle from both sides. A politician, Shindo has made frequent pilgrimages with Americans to Iwo Jima in order to foster friendship between the two nations, to learn more about what happened to his grandfather and countrymen, and to uncover and repatriate the bones of the dead. "They hid themselves on

PAPER LANTERNS FLOATED IN front of the Atomic Bomb Dome in Hiroshima on August 6, 2015, to mark the 70th anniversary of the bombing. The structure is one of the few buildings to survive the nuclear blast.

that fortress of an island and fought on alone to prolong the battle," Shindo said in a 2015 Reuters interview for the 70th anniversary of Iwo Jima. "They think they are still fighting, so I want to bring them home as soon as possible."

Even decades later, it has been hard for many to grapple with that seemingly buried past. President Bush long found it difficult to come to terms with his experience. "I wake up at night and think about it sometimes," he acknowledged of losing his two comrades in Chichi-jima. Like many, Bush admitted to harboring resentment for the Japanese and their emperor-god: "I had been taught that—an 18-, 19-year-old kid fighting for his country—that [Hirohito] was the epitome of all evil, he and Hitler." But with time that changed, and Bush was pleased with the transformation he witnessed in Japan. When Hirohito died in 1989, Bush attended his funeral in Tokyo.

Thirteen years later, Bush returned to Chichi-jima. There he retraced the route of his mission. "The waves and wind looked hauntingly familiar," the former President said. A launch then took him out to his crash site, beneath which rests his bomber. There he set two flower wreaths on the water for John Delaney and William "Ted" White, his comrades who died on that mission, and watched as the current took them away. After a ceremony on the island, Japanese onlookers waved American flags and cheered him.

Thankfully, people have not forgotten those long-ago battlefields, those who fought, those who gave their lives, and what started it all for America on that infamous day in 1941. The USS *Arizona* has never been raised. On Memorial Day in 1962, the USS *Arizona* Memorial was dedicated. Almost 2 million people visit the Pearl Harbor site each year. Many are young Japanese tourists sporting sunglasses and texting on their smartphones. At the memorial they can stand on the site where at 8:10 a.m. on December 7, 1941, a massive bomb devastated the *Arizona* and entombed 1,102 sailors below. The *Arizona*'s tanks still contain hundreds of thousands of gallons of oil. The fuel slowly leaks from its watery grave, and droplets rise to the surface. Often called the "Black Tears of the *Arizona*," they are a poignant reminder of what began at Pearl Harbor and then finally ended in Tokyo Bay 75 years ago. ●

Photo Credits

Front Cover: Joe Rosenthal/AP/Shutterstock **Back Cover:** Alfred Eisenstaedt/The LIFE Picture Collection/Getty **Page 1:** Press Association/O.W.I./National Archives **Pages 2–3:** U.S. Marines

INTRODUCTION
Pages 4–5: Bettmann/Getty

CHAPTER 1
Pages 6–7: US Navy/National Archives **Pages 8–9:** AP/Shutterstock **Pages 10–11** (clockwise from top): Keystone/Hulton/Getty; Bettmann/Getty; Ullstein Bild/Getty **Page 12:** Popperfoto/Getty **Page 13:** Ullstein Bild/Getty **Page 14** (from top): Time Life Pictures/US Navy/The LIFE Picture Collection/Getty; Archive Photos/Getty; U.S.S. Arizona Memorial/NPS **Page 15** (from top): Historical/Corbis/Getty; U.S. Navy **Pages 16–17:** The Granger Collection **Pages 18–19** (clockwise from top left): Time Life Pictures/National Archives/The LIFE Picture Collection/Getty; U.S. Navy (2) **Pages 20–21** (from left): AP/Shutterstock; Sherman Grinberg Film Library **Pages 22–23** (from left): Walter Sanders/Black Star; Bettmann/Getty **Pages 24–25:** Bettmann/Getty

CHAPTER 2
Pages 26–27: AP/Shutterstock **Pages 28–29:** Tsuguichi Koyanagi **Page 30:** National Archives **Page 31:** Bettmann/Getty **Pages 32–33:** Hansel Mieth/The LIFE Picture Collection/Getty (2) **Pages 34–35** (clockwise from top left): Herbert Gehr/The LIFE Images Collection/Getty; Bettmann/Getty; Anthony Potter Collection/Archive Photos/Getty **Pages 36–37** (from left): Hulton/Archive Photos/Getty; AP/Shutterstock **Pages 38–39** (from left): The Art Archive/Shutterstock; Universal History Archive/UIG/Getty **Pages 40–41** (from left): U.S. Marines; Ralph Morse/The LIFE Picture Collection/Getty **Pages 42–43:** George Strock/The LIFE Picture Collection/Getty (2) **Page 44:** Corbis/Getty **Page 45:** Bettmann/Getty **Pages 46–47:** U.S. Navy

CHAPTER 3
Pages 48–49: Jazz Editions/Gamma-Rapho/Getty **Page 50:** Everett/Shutterstock **Page 51:** US Navy/FPG/Archive Photos/Getty **Pages 52–53** (from left): Sgt. James L. Burns/US Marine Corps/The LIFE Picture Collection/Getty; W. Eugene Smith/The LIFE Picture Collection/Getty **Pages 54–55:** W. Eugene Smith/The LIFE Picture Collection/Getty (2) **Pages 56–57** (clockwise from top left): Kirn Vintage Stock/Corbis/Getty; PhotoQuest/Archive Photos/Getty; Cincinnati Museum Center/Archive Photos/Getty **Page 58:** Corbis/Getty **Page 59:** Carl Mydans/The LIFE Picture Collection/Getty **Pages 60–61** (from left): U.S. Army; Everett/Shutterstock **Pages 62–63** (clockwise from top): Carl Mydans/The LIFE Picture Collection/Getty; The Asahi Shimbun/Getty; Carl Mydans/The LIFE Picture Collection/Getty

CHAPTER 4
Pages 64–65 Universal History Archive/UIG/Getty **Pages 66–67:** US Signal Corps/The LIFE Picture Collection/Getty **Pages 68–69:** Carl Mydans/The LIFE Picture Collection/Getty (2) **Pages 70–71** (from left): W. Eugene Smith/The LIFE Picture Collection/Getty; Keystone/Hulton/Getty **Pages 72–73** (clockwise from top left): W. Eugene Smith/The LIFE Picture Collection/Getty; Universal History Archive/UIG/Getty; Everett/Shutterstock **Pages 74–75** (clockwise from top): George Eastman Museum/Premium/Getty; Prisma Bildagentur/UIG/Getty; Time Life Pictures/Wartime Japanese Govt./The LIFE Picture Collection/Getty **Pages 76–77** (clockwise from left): Corbis/Getty; Bettmann/Getty; U.S. Army **Page 78** (clockwise from top): George Skadding/The LIFE Picture Collection/Getty; William C. Shrout/The LIFE Picture Collection/Getty; Ed Clark/The LIFE Picture Collection/Getty **Page 79:** Gamma-Keystone/Getty **Page 80:** Rolls Press/Popperfoto/Getty **Page 81:** Corbis/Getty **Pages 82–83** (clockwise from top left): National Archives; Universal History Archive/UIG/Getty; Bernard Hoffman/The LIFE Picture Collection/Getty **Pages 84–85** (from top): Bettmann/Getty (2); Alinari/Getty **Pages 86–87:** Keystone/Hulton/Getty **Pages 88–89:** Eliot Elisofon/The LIFE Picture Collection/Getty

THE AFTERMATH
Pages 90–91 (from top): AP/Shutterstock; Margaret Bourke-White/The LIFE Picture Collection/Getty **Pages 92–93** (from top): Carl Mydans/The LIFE Picture Collection/Getty; Xinhua News Agency/Getty **Pages 94–95:** Kazuhiro Nogi/AFP/Getty **Page 96:** Kent Nishimura/Getty

HONORING THE HEROES

USS *Arizona* survivor Louis Conter saluted the *Arizona* remembrance wall during a 2015 service marking the Pearl Harbor attack. "People call us heroes," Conter said the following year. "We're not the heroes. The 1,177 who went down with the ship are the heroes. You have to remember, we got to go home, get married, have children and grandchildren, and we've lived a good life. Those who didn't get to do that should be called the heroes."

Printed in Dunstable, United Kingdom

66351651R00056